UNIVERSAL CHARACTER
EDUCATION

UNIVERSAL CHARACTER EDUCATION

Ian Bruce Kelsey, Ph.D.

THE PENTLAND PRESS LTD
EDINBURGH·CAMBRIDGE·DURHAM

First published in 1993 by
The Pentland Press Ltd.
1 Hutton Close
South Church
Bishop Auckland
Durham

ISBN 1 85821 050 X

Typeset by Spire Origination Ltd., Norwich
Printed and bound by Antony Rowe Ltd., Chippenham

It is the moral qualities of its leading personalities that are perhaps of even greater significance for a generation and for the course of history than purely intellectual accomplishments. Even these latter are, to a far greater degree than is commonly credited, dependent on the stature of character.

Albert Einstein

Permission granted by the Albert Einstein Archives, the Hebrew University of Jerusalem, Israel.

About the Author

Ian Bruce Kelsey is Chairman of the Vancouver School Board in Canada. He was educated in Canada, Scotland and America. He earned a bachelor's degree and a master's degree at the University of British Columbia and a doctorate in education (Ph.D.) at the University of Washington (Seattle).

The ideas expressed here are the product of the author's thirty-six years' immersion in the Canadian school system as a high school teacher, school administrator, college and university faculty member, university administrator, college board member and chairman, and school board member and chairman.

The ideas set forth in this book are intended as a manual for the establishment and maintenance of character education for children in the world's public school systems. The author feels the logic of events led him into education to discover, in his words, ''what education could and should do to develop individual potential for the benefit of the individual, of society, and of the world.''

Contents

Foreword

For those men and women who, in their casual or serious philosophical moods and moments, sometimes picture humanity as a mass of seafarers aboard the rudderless ''ship of progress'' tossing aimlessly in the ever-tumultuous sea of greed and lust; who find their minds trapped in ambivalence between the positive and negative aspects of the amazing advances of science and technology; who torment themselves by juxtaposing their thoughts about peace and war, about justice and injustice, about freedom and slavery, about democracy and authoritarianism, about hope and gloom: for them *Universal Character Education* offers a refreshingly concrete and practical plan to create the kind of humane, civilized and peaceful world society they yearn for.

This noble goal, according to Dr Ian Bruce Kelsey, author of this revolutionary book on education, is not unachievable. How then is it achieved? A world-wide public education system whose constituent members in every country uphold and pursue the philosophy of character development is the avenue, he claims.

The concept of character development as an educational philosophy is, of course, not new. Public education was established on this basis in many countries during the previous century. From that standpoint, therefore, Dr Kelsey's book is not a revolutionary work. However, considering the state of education on a world-wide basis today, Dr Kelsey's vision of a global or universal public education system based on character development makes his *Universal Character Education* very much a revolutionary piece of literature.

The public system envisaged by Dr Kelsey emphasizes as well as transcends personal virtues. It obliterates national boundaries, demolishes narrow nationalistic pride, sweeps away barriers of race, wealth or status and challenges the dogmatism of religion or ideology. It has one, and only one, purpose: to prepare the world's children to serve humanity.

These days the very mention of character education causes eyebrows to be raised in many circles, including school teachers. Some liberals, socialists, conservatives and religious groups have called character education a sinister agenda for the imposition of values. Such criticism is totally unjustified. The author, a highly experienced teacher, administrator and elected policy-maker, gives his unqualified support to the content of the academic, the athletic, the fine and performing arts, and the technological arts programmes in schools. High standards, generous accommodation for the average and below-average achievers, challenge for the gifted, discipline through a set of fair and firm rules and regulations are, in fact, striking features of his philosophy on character education for all. He fits easily into the category of the traditionalist — the dedicated professional teacher of a basic curriculum.

But the author, for whom spirituality is synonymous with love of the good and love of humanity, stands at a much higher plane of education than the efficient and skilful pedagogue. For him public education is far nobler and more extensive than simply ensuring that young people become good readers, writers, numerators and researchers. The skills and concepts learned through the school curriculum are tools which the young use to discover their potential in physical, social, creative, intellectual, emotional, moral and spiritual terms. They are intended to help the young during their adult life to become creative and thoughtful citizens of the world.

Education is meant to enlighten and civilize. Unfortunately public education, which has been diverted for so long from its original purpose of character development, caters more to mankind's baser nature than to its nobler side. Greed, profit, cut-throat competition in domestic and world markets, war needs, cast their long, dark shadows on modern education. The recurrence of two world wars in this century and over one hundred current wars makes one wonder whether modern education in general has achieved much in the way of civilizing the human race. To ensure a lasting peace on earth there is a great need for the emergence of a world leadership committed to the welfare of all human beings — a world leadership whose educational roots are in a world-wide public school system based on the philosophy of character development for the purpose of serving mankind.

The hope for mankind lies in a global non-sectarian educational system. And none is more suited than the educational model detailed by Dr Kelsey in his *Universal Character Education*. This model, which addresses all the educational needs of young people of all nations, will be easily acceptable to the governments of the world because its core curriculum, in terms of subject matter, remains the same as in modern education everywhere, even while its underlying philosophy and purpose are to prepare young people to serve the world.

It is possible, even likely, that Dr Kelsey's work will be received with scepticism by pedagogues and professional educators who have for long concentrated on promoting excellence in academics, athletics and the arts as the be all and end all of education, by followers of political and economic nationalism, by religious and cultural fanatics, by dictators and tyrants. The ordinary people, whose preoccupation is always with day to day social and economic concerns, may also fail to appreciate Dr Kelsey's vision. However, its relevance and significance cannot be missed by the small minority of thinkers who liken humanity to that proverbial group of innocent, aimless sailors aboard a rudderless ship.

Universal Character Education has perhaps appeared a quarter of a century ahead of its time. But the world is changing fast. The Cold War is officially at an end. Democracy is replacing totalitarianism in Eastern Europe. Democracy has blanketed all of South America and is spreading into Central America. White supremacy in South Africa has almost crumbled. The age of the superpowers is almost at a close. The new dynamics at the United Nations, particularly in the Security Council, bode well for peace and humanity. Interdependence, openness and closer communication among nations of the world will become the essential aspects of the emerging new internationalism. With that, of course, the shaping of a new world culture under the umbrella of the United Nations is *inevitable*.

Public education in conjunction with the United Nations Educational, Scientific and Cultural Organization (UNESCO) will play a major role in developing a common cultural web for mankind. During this period of educational and cultural metamorphosis, leaders in the international community will turn to the educational model provided by Dr Kelsey with enthusiasm and gratitude because they will find within his vision of a global public school system for character education the key to make this planet a peaceful, strife-free home.

Universal Character Education belongs to all mankind. Let the light of it begin to reach out into every corner of the globe.

Harkirpal S. Sara, BA, MA
Retired Teacher and
Former Vancouver (Canada)
School Board Member

Preface

After years of wandering in the wilderness of public education, I came to the conclusion that all education is character education — that is, the elevation of character. I arrived at this conclusion through experience, observation, reason, insight and intuition. I did not consult with others, examine relevant literature, or visit schools and programmes claiming to advance character education. I discovered solely through my own travels and travails that the path of a sound education leads to the same destination for all — freedom — freedom from limitation and freedom to use God-reflected talents and abilities without inhibition or dissimulation. That freedom dawns over many years as individuals work out their own destiny, and come to realize they have an obligation to contribute to the betterment of society and the world. This education leads to the uncovering of potential, often hidden or unknown, and to self-government. It leads to humility, mildness and power. It leads to vitality and activity. It leads to regenerative interludes of solitude and stillness. It leads to unselfishness and responsibility, to a life of giving, sharing, contributing, a life of productivity and prosperity. It leads in sum to undivided freedom.

There is no mystery to character education. It is a conscious, disciplined daily effort to follow school practices that produce the educated citizen. This individual has been identified as an independent thinker, a problem-solver, a producer, a doer; someone who is principled, thoughtful, respectful, cooperative; someone who is flexible, imaginative, creative; someone who exhibits moral courage and gratitude; someone who is fearless, confident, bold. Growth in these attributes occurs as the individual willingly follows the direction and inspiration provided by teachers and mentors. Growth occurs gradually over the years as one winds one's way through academics, athletics, the arts and other activities offered within a nation's schools.

The key to this growth is the individual's own receptivity to the teaching provided by those schools. But that growth is enhanced by the quality of the teachers the individual has over many years. It is essential therefore that those teachers be of the highest calibre possible in terms of character and that *all* who work in those schools be of a similar calibre.

Set forth in the following pages are the essential elements in that education, an education that makes for a healthy individual, a strong country, and a civilized society — an open, free, progressive, diverse and democratic society. It is the right of all children throughout the world to benefit from the elevation of character that can take place in a democratic public school system established by the people for the people. All children are born free; public universal character education will ensure their freedom forever.

Chapter 1

Philosophy

The belief that every school or educational system needs its own philosophy is wrong. There can be only one statement of fundamental belief for the education of children because education should be the same wherever it takes place. It should be basically the same in London, Belfast, Dublin, Jerusalem, Baghdad, Moscow, Berlin, Rome, New York, Montreal, Vancouver, Tahsis, Darwin, Beijing, Tokyo, Peshawar, Bombay, Cairo, Johannesburg, Buenos Aires, Quito, Managua or wherever. The same quality of education is possible in village, town or city. Quality education transcends surroundings, be those rural or urban, and can lift the individual out of debilitating elements, perceived or real.

The need for educated individuals is the same the world over. The need is for individuals to realize, to actualize, their potential for good. It is just as true for our neighbour's children as it is for our own. It is true for children of parents who identify themselves as Catholic, Protestant, Sikh, Jew, Muslim, Bahai, Zoroastrian, Hindu, Buddhist, Jainist, humanist, atheist, agnostic. It is true for children of the rich and children of the poor; it is true for the advantaged and the disadvantaged; it is true for the able and the disabled; it is true for boys and girls; it is true for the gifted and the non-gifted; it is true for African, Oriental, Caucasian, Aboriginal. The need is universal and always will be.

Every country needs a healthy society, a society that hums with activity and vitality. That in turn generates a vibrant economy where new ideas and practices result in increased circulation of goods and

1

services and monies. Change becomes the constant and the old is regenerated or replaced by the new. Expectancy welcomes the new and is glad to leave the outworn and obsolete. This does not lessen an affection and attachment to fixed principles and does not weaken family and community ties. It strengthens them by looking for new ways to further their richness. An emphasis is placed not so much on the material aspect of change as on the more spiritual, the intangibles that create and stabilize change, intangibles such as honesty, openness, freshness. This does not throw off older people; it encourages regeneration throughout life and makes use of ageless talents and abilities. It leads to ageless societies where individuals are noted not for their age but for their on-going contribution to the world.

The educated citizen is essential for every nation. Each nation prospers or declines depending upon the education of its children. Civil, religious, political, legislative, judicial and economic reforms continue only through that education. The future of humanity lies, therefore, not with adults but with children and their proper education. Children always will be the hope of humanity; education always will be the avenue through which that hope can come to fruition.

Education in its purest form is a gradual process of awakening individuals to their unlimited potential for accomplishing good. It is unhurried, unpressured, unfettered. It is not unlike the unfolding of the petals in a flower. It simply requires the right atmosphere and nutrients. Nature supplies those for the flower; teachers and parents supply those for the child.

The awakening occurs through growth in all facets of the individual's make-up or being. This make-up has been termed the whole person. While many have recommended educating this whole person, few have actually done so because the whole has never been clearly and specifically identified. Most thinkers have limited their whole to the physical, mental and social dimensions of an individual. Others have included the emotional or creative or moral realms. A few have included the spiritual. And fewer still have included all these facets of an individual's being. As a result, the curriculum in almost all public schools has been designed to encourage growth in only a few of these

2

dimensions, and often with exclusive focus on intellectual growth. Progress of children and predictions of their success have been based almost solely on intellectual performance. Generations of children have suffered from this narrow focus.

It is not intellectual development alone that governs individual, national and global progress. It is the unleashing of individual potential in all its varied manifestations that does that.

So real education is the unlocking of potential. And that potential can be released only as the school addresses the individual from the perspective of the whole person. That whole includes the mental, physical, emotional, social, creative, moral and spiritual dimensions of every child.

These dimensions are not discrete. They blend with each other within every individual. And within every individual some facets are more highly developed than others. Development here is always individual. It is an on-going, life-time process. Foundation for the growth begins in the home and is reinforced in the school. Growth beyond that continues only through individual initiative.

Fulfilment of potential is dependent solely upon the individual's continuing growth in all facets of human individuality. Growth is never-ending; fulfilment is never-ending. Both are always relative — relative to where one was, one is, and where one is pushing towards in terms of expression of the qualities related to the spiritual, moral, mental, emotional, physical, social and creative dimensions of existence. In the school setting children are helped in that growth and fulfilment through example, encouragement, effort and receptivity.

Every child is always at a different level of expression of these dimensions from every other child. It is the parent's responsibility and the teacher's job to discern as well as possible those levels and to encourage each child to build upon and enlarge that expression. That building or enlarging is the growth that occurs in freeing the individual to use his or her potential.

As principal of a combined elementary and secondary school (Kindergarten — 12th Grade), I developed with teachers a philosophy that would state clearly the comprehensive nature of what education for

3

every one of our children should be. I believe it provides a sound new direction to the education of children throughout the world. The substance of that philosophy is found in the following statement.

All education is character education. That is, every facet of schooling is designed to aid in the total development of the individual.

This development includes growth in the spiritual, moral, emotional, intellectual, social, physical and creative realms. The spiritual refers to cultivation of a love of good in any form, with emphasis on love of one another; moral refers to an awareness of right and wrong and a willingness to act in accord with one's highest sense of right; emotional refers to the expression and control of feelings, sensitivity to the feelings of others and a consideration of those feelings; intellectual refers to cultivation of things of the mind and an ability to think for oneself; social refers to the ability and willingness to interact with others on a wholesome basis; physical refers to participation in wholesome, vigorous physical activities; and creative refers to cultivation of an attitude that promotes fresh approaches to problems and their solution.

All activities carried on in the school, from the purely academic through the artistic to the broadly practical, contribute to growth in these dimensions.

Major responsibility for this growth rests with the home, but the school supports this growth by providing an atmosphere and activities which, when undertaken seriously and conscientiously by the student, contribute strongly to this growth. This growth is, in the final analysis, the development of character.

This development is what enables our students to become confident, considerate and intelligent contributors to the country and the world. And that contribution will be in any areas students elect, one no less important than any other.

This philosophy or statement of fundamental belief should be the same for every school throughout the world. It becomes a permanent, solid foundation for the school and for every activity carried on by the school. Like a rock, it will not wear away with waves of change and time. Children, parents, teachers, administrators, support staff, buildings, grounds, facilities, technology, resources and curriculum come and go; but the one single all-encompassing philosophy remains to benefit each new generation of children.

This philosophy can be effective only if all teachers, administrators and support staff accept it and uphold it. Those who do not, undermine the effectiveness of those working to support it. Factions develop and students are torn between conflicting directions and practices.

Parents should also be supportive of the philosophy. Most will be. Experience has shown me, however, that not all will be. Some will be supportive in word only. A few will work against it, either ignorantly or intentionally. That cannot be avoided and should not interfere with the school's single-minded approach to education of the whole child. Parents should not be allowed into any public school under the guise of volunteering or assisting and then sow seeds of criticism about its administration and teaching. Teachers and administrators have to cut off this destructive head of criticism the moment it appears. Constructive discussion is healthy for the school and system; destructive criticism is unhealthy, and eventually nullifies the elevation of character being furthered by the school. While major responsibility for the growth of the child rests with the home, especially in preparing the child to be receptive for learning, the home can seldom replace the education provided by the school.

One of the most challenging tasks teachers and administrators face is maintaining an atmosphere which contributes to the total education of the children in their charge. It is a continuous challenge because there is always some individual, group or agency that wants its own ideas spread within the system. Some even want to monitor what goes on within the school and change the school's approach to conform to their ideal of a school. That should never be permitted. Public schools do not exist for the personal whims and fancies of any special interest group or individual. They exist for the freeing of individual potential. Parents and others not trained in that freeing are frequently mistaken on how best to bring that about. So teachers need to guard against the breaking down of their efforts and responsibilities to educate the whole child.

Parents should take their children to school and leave them there alone with the teachers and administrators trained to educate them. And where teachers and administrators are not doing their job of educating the whole child, they should be encouraged to seek employment in fields other than education. Education is the keystone in the progress of nations. It requires the employment therefore of only those with a deep affection for children and a commitment to the philosophy of character education that when properly applied frees the young to use their potential for the advancement of the world.

Chapter 2

Standards for Teachers

In character education there can be only one kind of teacher. This teacher has to be a model of outstanding character. This person must have a history of patience, affection, enthusiasm, thoughtfulness, respectfulness, flexibility, imagination, firmness, intelligence, good judgment and confidence. This individual, like the educated citizen, must be a thinker, a problem-solver, a producer, a doer. This person must have demonstrated staying power and accomplishment. While accomplishment is important in academics, the arts, athletics and practical fields, any taint of arrogance, aloofness, argumentativeness or domination of others disqualifies anyone from entry into teaching.

Teachers teach what they are. Their mental states, like their life-styles, influence their students more than all their intellect and abilities. Behind the mask of many a pleasant disposition lies mental, emotional and moral deformity. That manifests itself as deceit, dishonesty, assertiveness, arrogance, sensualism, and an unhealthy ambition for power, position and recognition. That is what is transmitted to students, not the disposition.

The mask of pleasantness deludes the innocent and leads many an unsuspecting child into patterns of thought and activity which are harmful to his or her growth. Many of these deluded young people never do gain release from those patterns which bind them to limitations. Some are mentally, emotionally, morally or socially crippled for a life-time. So it is not a pleasant personality that is needed; it is an individual who is a pattern for decency, reasonableness, and fairness, for innocence, purity, and wholesomeness. Teachers serve as models for a nation; the importance of that modelling can never be over-emphasized. All teachers, without exception, have to cultivate the qualities that make for the truly educated citizen.

Growth in this cultivation continues while the teacher is on the job. But there must have been evidence of the exercise of the qualities before entry into teaching. It is the job of every faculty of education at an accredited degree-granting college or university to screen carefully every teacher applicant. This screening must be more rigorous than that conducted for entry into any other field. It must include interviews of candidates, interviews of those who are familiar with their work or activities, and interviews of others acquainted with their growth and development. Mental and emotional stability must be clearly apparent and moral and spiritual growth evident. This is best determined by those familiar with each applicant's work and background. It should be obvious, but has to be made indelibly clear, that those doing the screening must themselves be of outstanding character.

If qualities of the educated citizen are not clearly apparent during training and professional development, the applicant should not be certified to teach.

Except in emerging or developing countries, where advanced education has not yet progressed to a significantly high level, admission to a faculty of education should be confined to those who have a bachelor's degree. This ensures an adequate level of academic development for entry into teaching. Developing countries will have to grow to that level of entry gradually as their populace becomes better educated and there is a sufficient supply of qualified teachers.

Scholarship is important in every teacher. The crucial element in the selection of a teacher in any country, however, is the quality of the applicant. Without quality, character development in public schools is possible in name only. The brightest and most accomplished individual may be a wicked person. That is not the kind of individual a country should be seeking for its teaching staff. It is only the best in terms of character that every country can afford to have educating — elevating — its children and young people.

Chapter 3

Standards for Students

Although I have had over twenty years of teaching experience, virtually all at the high school and university levels, and have seen many students go on to what appears to be productive lives, I have never been satisfied with the focus of that teaching. Emphasis was always on achievement and performance, largely academic. Measurement of progress was based primarily on knowledge and skills, with some judgment on work habits. These are important elements of education and have their rightful place. But that place is always secondary to growth in character.

Character is the blending and manifestation of qualities that comprise the individual. There are as many combinations of those qualities as there are individuals — literally billions. Every person individualizes the qualities in different ways. The individualization of these qualities should result ultimately, regardless of their combinations, in peace, goodwill and love for all. Out of that arises progress and prosperity for individuals and then nations.

In many cases that is not the result, and in far too many instances the results are the opposite — war, violence and hatred. Why? Because too many individuals are motivated by lust for power, prestige and position, by the desire for supremacy over others, by a drive to be the greatest. It is an all-consuming drive of self-love. That drive can never be satisfied. Individuals who exercise this kind of lust, desire and drive are uneducated. They may have attended school, college or university, but they have not been educated. They have not been freed from slavery to their own self-centredness. They have yet to learn that the universal qualities accessed by mankind must always be used for the advancement of humanity and in the interests of humanity. This includes intelligence, intuition, wisdom, justice, mercy, compassion, love, vitality, perseverance, patience, hope, faith, trust, teachableness, mildness, humility.

The exercise of these qualities enables individuals to see things from the perspective of another's position, to work alongside others in spite of differences, to compromise, to refuse to react to displays of resentment, animosity or disdain, to be patient with their own and others' shortcomings, to see things through to a successful conclusion. These qualities are the substance of human activity and ultimately the prime determiners of success in all human affairs. Assessment of the expression of these qualities through the domains of the mental, emotional, physical, social, creative, moral and spiritual will show clearly each student's actual educational progress. This assessment is always subjective, but it determines more effectively than measurement of intellectual abilities the possibility of success in contributing to the welfare of the community and the world.

This does not mean the abandonment of teaching for high levels of intellectual achievement and performance. Nor does it mean the abandonment of assessing achievement and performance. That assessment should continue. But the focus should shift from primarily intellectual achievement and measurement to the cultivation or expression of the qualities identified. Paradoxically, experience shows that one of the results of that shift is enhanced achievement in all activities, academic as well as artistic, athletic or practical. The individual gradually becomes accustomed to the exercise of the qualities and eventually lets the results take care of themselves. The focus shifts gradually from performance or achievement to *living of the qualities*.

All schools are nurseries of character. They are places where individual growth takes place gradually over many years. It cannot be rushed or accelerated. It is not the work of any one moment. It is the work of moments put together, one after the other. All those moments need to be carefully guarded so that there is no disruption of the growth that is taking place. It is essential therefore that the behaviour of students be carefully monitored by firm teachers and administrators.

Where there is disruption of learning, that disruption must be stopped immediately. This can normally be handled by the individual teacher. Where that is not possible or is not being done, and I have witnessed such situations, the administration needs to remove the individual student or students and ensure that they do not return to the learning situation until there is assurance that no further disruption will occur. Removal may be within the school or it may be without. If students need to be sent home, that must be done. If privileges need to be denied, that too must be done. Physical restraint may be necessary in cases of severe behaviour problems, but physical punishment in any form should never occur; neither should yelling, screaming and shouting. No berating, admonishing or cajoling of students in front of others should ever take place. Discipline should be consistently firm, decisive and swift, but never humiliating or abusive. The dignity of the child or young person being disciplined must always be upheld, even in the most difficult of cases. A sound guide in all cases of discipline is to encourage teachers and administrators to act as they would if they were kind, firm and judicious parents. Character cannot be elevated by brute force or intimidation.

In some severe behaviour cases police officers may have to be called upon to ensure the safety of students and staff, but these cases should be rare. These are not educational issues; they are criminal, and as such require legal and police support for their initial handling. Crime must be checked immediately. Once that has been accomplished, rehabilitation and reformation can begin. The latter cannot precede the former.

In all schools and in all school districts procedures need to be established for the orderly handling of discipline cases. These procedures should include provision for deprivation of privileges, removal from activities on a temporary or long-term basis, class suspension, school suspension, transfer to another district school if possible, and eventually expulsion from school after all efforts to assist and encourage reformation of character have been exhausted.

There has been far too much leniency on the part of schools, at least on the North American continent, with disruptive students. That has led to poor learning situations for far too many students and therefore little growth in character development. Society has had to suffer from this leniency with students coming out of schools ill-prepared to contribute to society. This has nothing to do with lack of knowledge, skill development, career or job training; it has everything to do with character development.

Where students fail to fit in with school rules and regulations, they should be directed to work with school counsellors, social workers, psychologists, health officers, and others in the community to help them improve their behaviour. There should be cooperation between the home, school and community personnel, but there must not be a return to school until that behaviour has indeed been improved. Age of students is not a factor. Disruption at any age is unacceptable. Academic and practical studies can still continue outside the school setting, but character development is impossible until there is receptivity and a willingness to meet school requirements in terms of conduct. The basic purpose of the school is always elevation of character. Conduct and behaviour are vital parts of that elevation.

While many people feel education is a continuous process from birth to death, and different countries establish differing starting and leaving ages for formal education, my own view is that institutional education is not necessary before six years of age. Education is going on before this, but it is more informal and incidental than that provided in a school setting. Parents should provide the direction for the children almost entirely prior to this age. Parents the world over should resist the pressures that inevitably accompany evolving complex technological and service societies to speed up the formal schooling of their children. Childhood is a time in large measure for freedom from formality and highly structured institutions. It is a time for play and wholesome enjoyment of nature and home. And no instruction is needed in the basics of reading, writing and mathematics except in naturally incidental ways. The most important thing for young children is to feel the love that only caring parents and family can provide. This comes primarily from healthy, stable marriages.

No student should remain in public school beyond the age of nineteen. The school cannot help shape the character of individuals beyond that age. Each individual has to assume that responsibility alone from that point on. Academic or career development continues with further formal work, but character development continues only with individual initiative.

I have seen many students linger in senior high school for academic and social reasons, but that lingering has almost always delayed their development. It served primarily to reinforce previous patterns of thinking and behaviour. That is not progress for the individual or for society.

The popular belief that students and society benefit from retaining in school those who do not want to be there, who refuse to learn, and who attend only because the law insists they attend, is a belief without substance. In reality few of these individuals do profit, and society seldom. In the meantime many other students have suffered from their presence and adverse influence, with teachers expending time and energy futilely encouraging them to fit into the standards set for all.

The root of the problem with recalcitrant students is insubordination. Insubordination is an evil. It obstructs self-development. It eventually has to be dissolved. And that can be accomplished only by identifying the problem, acknowledging it as a problem, and then reasoning through to see its obstructive nature and the necessity for its dissolution. That is not easy to do, but must be done before there is any hope of progress, even for young children.

The basic problem with insubordination is that individuals affected have never learned from their parents, their parent substitutes, or their teachers, to be receptive to the guidance provided throughout their childhood or teenage years. Self-will has dominated thoughts, feelings and actions for so long that they have not been able to subordinate those to higher, more selfless thoughts, feelings and actions. As a result these individuals have had great difficulty accepting instruction, guidance or direction. Cooperation with anyone but themselves has been almost impossible.

Insubordination is not incurable, but there can be no growth out of its adverse influence until the individual affected sees the necessity for growth. That often comes only after years of suffering and, on rare occasions, through reflective thought or insight. Until that necessity appears such individuals should be encouraged to complete their studies at centres, institutions, and places where receptivity, conduct and behaviour are not key factors in their progress. Distance learning networks, correspondence schools, local colleges and some private training institutes may well suit these students. Character growth for these individuals is best left to individual necessity.

In the world's public schools there is then only one acceptable standard for all students. That standard is receptivity to the direction given by teachers in terms of conduct, behaviour and seriousness towards school work, studies and activities. The school must insist on this standard at all times. As it does, student progress will be apparent in all facets of school life.

Chapter 4

Curriculum

The public school curriculum should be basically the same everywhere in the world. Curriculum is content. It is what students study and take part in to guide their growth in all facets of character development. It is only in the more senior levels of high school that distinct changes in that curriculum should occur. And those changes should be minimal.

Coupled with the basic curriculum is the construction of school buildings to ensure children of similar age groups study, play and work together in an atmosphere which contributes to their wholesome growth. The best arrangement for optimal character development is to group into one set of buildings children from five or six years of age to ten; group into another set of buildings those from eleven years of age to thirteen; and group into the third set those from fourteen years of age to eighteen. These schools can be termed the Primary School, Middle School and High School respectively. Grade designations are Kindergarten or Grade 1 through Grade 5; Grade 6 through Grade 8; Grade 9 through Grade 12.

Although these distinct divisions result in higher capital, operating, and maintenance costs, they need to be made for the benefit of the children. The primary benefit is in ensuring an atmosphere which is appropriate for each distinct age group. In these divisions children are in constant contact with those of their own age group and interests. This encourages children to remain children as long as possible, an essential element in the development of character.

In some countries and in some isolated areas with small populations these divisions may not be practical or possible. All the children in such communities may have to be educated together in one set of buildings (even Kindergarten–12 or 1–12). That is a practical matter that has to be determined by state and local authorities. It needs to be kept in mind, however, that the divisions identified here provide the best physical arrangement for the different age groups. It also needs to be remembered that there is nothing going on within a community, isolated or non-isolated, small or large, more important to that community and to the world than the education of its children, so provision for that education should be the first priority within every community. If school divisions as identified here are possible within a community, strong efforts should be made to arrange for appropriate buildings.

Pressure from popular opinion will inevitably be brought to bear upon those responsible for the governance of public schools to admit children younger than five years of age. Many parents claim their children are ready for entry into school. That pressure should be resisted. My experience shows that the later the entry into the formal curriculum, even up to seven or eight years of age, depending upon the child, the easier the transition from home to school. This is especially so for the child who has been immersed in love and affection and provided with a stimulating home atmosphere. Even where these are lacking, school cannot completely overcome that lack. Entry into school at an early date only compounds that lack and often adds to the difficulties for the child lacking affection and care. Caring day care centres can help overcome that lack to some degree and are better than the school setting in the early years as they should not be working from the more formalized learning situation as found in school. These centres should foster love and affection, without a structured curriculum.

It is my view that entry into school should take place at only one time of the school year for all students. Dual entry (at the beginning of a school term or halfway through a term) or continuous entry (monthly entry or birth date entry) are detrimental, as relationships are usually stabilized at an early stage of each school term. Even school transfers during the school year tend to upset those relationships, relationships so vital to children in their early and late childhood years.

It is also my view that the first year of school, whether at five years of age or six, should be a full day. The full day should be introduced gradually from three hours a day to five within the first two months of school. Children readily adapt to routine and even at five years of age are capable of adjusting to the full day. For the few children who find the day too long, exceptions should be made to give them partial days.

It needs to be made clear to parents that children do not necessarily need to enter Kindergarten. The majority of children can readily enter school directly into Grade 1 at six years of age. Schools are not baby-sitting agencies. The more time children spend in a loving, enriching home with their parents prior to entering school, the richer the school experience.

The content or curriculum for Kindergarten children should be centred on wholesome activity. This should include an abundance of music and dance and art and running, leaping, skipping, climbing and talking, being read to, story-telling and visiting local areas, television viewing, radio listening, and an abundance of affection-sharing with the teacher.

Development along spiritual, moral, emotional, social, physical, mental and creative lines occurs if there is a conscious focus on these by the teacher. At this stage almost exclusive contact with adults is not beneficial to children. It tends to move them out of childhood at too early a stage. And there is no need to force children to read. They grow into the ability to read at approximately seven or eight years of age. Some children will not be ready even then. Those who blossom later than others often develop highly developed skills and abilities in their own time. I met a thirteen-year-old recently who was reading at the college level who had not learned to read until she was ten years of age. An excellent teacher of English told me she herself did not learn to read until she was eight years of age. It cannot be emphasized enough that children should not be forced to read before they are ready to do so.

The curriculum for children for Grade 1 to Grade 5, another distinct formative period, should focus on the children's national language and on basic mathematics. Other areas of study and activity should include local history and geography, science, fine and performing arts, and physical activity. Language includes all facets of communication, such as listening, speaking, reading and writing. Local field trips enrich and broaden views even at this age if there is an educational focus. Contact and work with computers and other technology are also beneficial as they help build a familiarity and ease with technology at an early age. Technological skill is not the aim, rather familiarity and comfort with technology. Twenty-five hours of instruction per week is adequate for children at this level. No home study is needed.

A second language that all students study should be introduced in the first year (Grade 6) of the Middle School. Study of it should continue until Grade 11. It should be primarily conversational. In countries where English is not the first language, English should be the second language. It will continue indefinitely to be the universal language in commerce, diplomacy, law, politics, medicine, culture, communications and education. Children without English will be at a disadvantage on the global scene. In countries where English is the first language, the second language of study will depend upon national and state preferences. Aboriginal or native or heritage languages may well meet the local need in this area.

The curriculum for children in Grades 6, 7 and 8 (the Middle School years) should focus on distinct subject areas. These subjects are the same as in the Primary School: first language, history, geography, mathematics, science, fine and performing arts, and physical activity. The only addition is the second language. There is always some overlapping and intertwining of these areas, with some jurisdictions encouraging integration of many of the subjects so there is a blending of areas. This has been done through the study of topics, themes, or major ideas, looking at them from the perspective of the humanities, sciences, practical or fine and performing arts. This approach may meet the need of some students for a comprehensive or interdisciplinary view, but it is my view that at this level and even into High School the best approach for the furtherance of knowledge and skills is to concentrate on distinct subjects rather than to blend them. As students develop analytical abilities, they naturally do their own interdisciplinary blending. Themes and contrived projects are not needed to encourage this.

School organization for the Middle School should be subject-based, similar to High School with the exception that it should not be semestered. Year-long seven or eight subject instruction is more beneficial for this age level than the more fragmented High School instruction. It provides for longer time with fewer teachers. Again, twenty-five hours per week of instruction is adequate in a 195-instructional day school year. If home study is needed, no more than sixty minutes per day should be assigned.

In Grades 9 through 12 (the High School years) all students, regardless of intellectual proficiency, need exposure and immersion in seven broad areas. These include the national language (4 years); history and geography (3 years); mathematics (3 years); science (3 years); a second language (3 years); fine and performing arts (3 years); and physical education (3 years). As well, elective or optional subjects should be offered in all four High School years in practical areas such as business, home economics, technical studies, computer studies, and the arts.

All students need academic subjects all their school days. Exposure to ideas and views brought out in these disciplines, especially in the humanities, is essential for development of the whole person. Depth of examination varies widely from one student to the next, but examination and exposure are imperative for expansion of thought. Students with little interest in academics and more interest in the practical, artistic or vocational can study and acquire skills and knowledge in these latter areas, but need to accompany that with purely academic studies. Work experience, pre-employment and career programmes are not substitutes for academic studies. Non-academically inclined students have just as important views and feelings on significant issues as do academically inclined students. In some cases they have more advanced views and feelings on issues demanding fairness, justice, mercy and compassion than do others. They need the opportunity and skills to bring these out for public benefit. The least articulate today may become the most advanced thinkers of tomorrow. These individuals often spend years struggling to articulate their innermost thoughts and feelings, so they need all the encouragement society can give them at each stage of their growth. Public schools should be the principal avenue for that encouragement in those early stages.

At this level instruction should be given for thirty hours per week — six hours per day for five days. All High Schools should operate on the semester system, enabling students to take twelve courses over a two-semester year. This will allow them to take forty-eight courses over the four years of high school. Acceleration through the system should not be permitted. The basic purpose of education is not academic, artistic, athletic or practical acceleration and achievement; it is character development. And that is impossible to accelerate. Home study should be no more than ninety minutes per day in the first two years and no more than one hundred and twenty minutes per day in the final two years. A school year of 195 instructional school days is adequate for all.

Textbooks for the basic curriculum should be of the highest calibre possible at each level. High standards of journalism should be maintained and literature at each level selected that elevates rather than titillates and trivializes. Arguments that some students are incapable of dealing with ideas from high level literature and art are unfounded. They will take from those ideas what meets their needs, and that will come back to them years later when needed. Shakespeare's observation that ''a friendly eye could never see such faults'' has just as much relevance in the market-place as it has on the floor of the United Nations, and is just as relevant to the common person today as it was when written centuries ago.

Textbooks, workbooks, manuals, curriculum guides and other resource materials, especially in the sciences, need constant up-dating to keep abreast of the times. It should be the responsibility of state ministries of education to ensure such up-dating on at least a ten-year cycle, with at least one curriculum area up-graded each year. Videos, cassettes, compact discs, computer software and hardware, shortwave radio, and technologies not yet invented must all be kept abreast of contemporary thought and practice. Students need the latest in ideas and practices so they remain on the cutting edge of world changes.

Modification of curricula may be appropriate in some cases. This should be done primarily to encourage and enable students to grow from a disadvantaged position to a higher level of thought and expression. The modification is not to replace the higher level course. The higher level course should be undertaken if and when the student is prepared to do so. Individuals with severe learning disabilities should never have placed upon them limits to their capabilities. No one knows when or under what conditions they will burst forth in all their beauty and ability. The expectation and opportunity to do so must always be present, and wherever possible their education should take place alongside all other students.

Curricula for the gifted, those who show peculiar gifts for learning either academically, artistically, athletically or technologically, should be similar to that for all students, with the added provision of the opportunity to explore and work with ideas and practices that challenge their special abilities.

Of all the areas within education that have proved to be a challenge, none has been more of a challenge or more vexing than the provision of appropriate learning experiences for gifted children and young people. I have witnessed and heard about more disasters with the gifted, and particularly the intellectually gifted, than with all other students combined. I believe the basic problem in this area has been the belief that what these individuals need is more of what they are particularly good at. The result has been from my perspective an imbalance in development with far too much emphasis on only one or two areas, and a corresponding lack of development in other dimensions to include the spiritual, moral, emotional, mental, physical, social and creative aspects of individuality.

Parents, teachers and administrators have repeatedly insisted that these students should be accelerated through the curriculum. Achievement and test scores have shown them that these individuals are superior to others in performance and ability in mathematics, the sciences or language. The solution, it has been claimed, is to advance them to higher levels of the same content, to challenge and enrich them to help keep them from boredom. This practice is still widely recommended and used. I am convinced that that practice is detrimental to the gifted, and especially the intellectually gifted. It fails to encourage development of the total individual.

What actually happens, I believe, when children and young people are pushed or pulled outside their chronological growth pattern, nature's pattern for them, is forced development with performance at a high level in the forced area or areas, but with a lag in development in the remaining areas. Those areas are neglected or ignored unconsciously and suffer as a result. The pressure for more advanced performance quickly becomes self-imposed and subtle. It is seen by no one, only felt by the child or young person. The individual feels high levels of achievement are expected and therefore silently struggles to satisfy the expectations. The individual gives the appearance of performing naturally, but inwardly there is the struggle of keeping up with expectations, never certain that what he or she is doing is correct or appropriate.

These experiences are premature. The child or young person has not grown emotionally, socially, creatively, morally, spiritually, or even physically, at the same rate as forced intellectual growth has taken place. The imbalance eventually results in disaster for the individual. Some individuals in this situation are overcome by their inability to cope with emotional issues, personal relationships, moral dilemmas, spiritual ignorance, creative vacuums. Some of them are overwhelmed by self-doubt, discouragement and depression, give up struggling to gain their dominion over these burdensome feelings, and fail to use their remarkable abilities at the level they are capable of exercising them. A number become satisfied with performing menial tasks simply for peace of mind and feelings. Others commit suicide because they have been unable to cope with demands and expectations placed upon them which they feel they cannot fulfil. Others simply go on indefinitely advancing intellectually but never having control over events and situations on an emotional, social, creative, moral or spiritual basis.

Intellectual development does not guarantee the ability to deal with things other than on an intellectual level. And intellect is not the key factor in dealing with life's everyday affairs. The key factors are spiritual and moral: what is right, what is wrong, what is neither right nor wrong, what is good, what is bad, what is neither good nor bad. The spiritual and moral show to us the need for development of the intellect, but the intellect does not tell us of the need for development of the spiritual and moral. Quite to the contrary, it argues solely for its own self-importance without any need for spiritual and moral considerations. This is a major reason why so many adults with a highly developed intellect cannot bring to the world solutions that demand moral courage, justice, bravery, mercy or compassion.

One of the truly damaging effects of accelerating the gifted is leaving them with the impression that they have capacities and abilities that set them apart from humanity. This is a horrible belief to inflict upon a child or young person because the effect is to separate them from others with the delusion that they are superior to others. From a spiritual standpoint nothing could be farther from the truth: all have the capacity to express in their own individual ways the infinite capacities of God. That fact has to be proved in everyday human activity, but the lack of its manifestation does not lessen the fact. It always remains for proving, demonstrating, manifesting.

Forced academic, artistic, athletic or career acceleration is somewhat similar to cutting open the cocoon surrounding the larva. It destroys the organism's ability to strengthen itself by winding its own way out of the cocoon. It eventually dies before reaching its ultimate state as a beautiful butterfly. Every individual needs to wind his or her own way through the challenges faced in daily affairs from a complete perspective. This strengthens the individual gradually, slowly, powerfully.

Every accelerated student I have been familiar with — over thirty — has failed to achieve anywhere near his or her potential as a result of an imbalance in development. All of them were unwittingly encouraged to concentrate on only one or two dimensions of their individuality.

As a result of their fragility the gifted need more assistance in the curriculum than any other group. They have as individuals more to contend with than others. They have a perceptiveness that enables them to focus almost instantly on the core of a problem and see possible solutions. They do not have to sort through all the paraphernalia — the flotsam and jetsam — that invariably surround complex issues. This ability places them in demand wherever they go. More is expected of them than it is of others. Their uniqueness tends to isolate them. Others frequently avoid them because they do not readily fit in with the often tedious and drawn-out mental wrestling that goes on with less perceptive individuals. These gifted individuals therefore usually have a lonely path to walk all their days. They often seek out friends who are less than sterling because they are a relief from the demands placed upon them. This in itself leads to great danger as some are readily led into situations they would not normally choose had they developed in a more balanced manner. A highly developed moral sense, for example, would have given them the mechanism to protect themselves from delicious but potentially dangerous situations.

These children and young people do need relief from incessant expectations and demands. It is, therefore, not more challenges in their own fields such as the academic or artistic or athletic or career preparation they need, but more compassion, more affection, more understanding, more acceptance of their uniqueness, more solitude, more time for their own thoughts, more time to reflect upon things of their own interest.

In terms of the school curriculum, then, these students do not need the extra stimulation so many claim they do. It is actually the less than gifted who need that. The gifted stimulate themselves with their own thoughts. The best thing in the curriculum for them is time to explore, to reflect upon, and to examine in more depth, the things other students are studying or examining. Knowledge and skills they quickly pick up with others. They can be given time on their own to explore or generate ideas in projects or papers beyond what others are doing if *they* feel the need. Exploration in the school library, study of another language, enrolment in correspondence courses or distance learning, immersion in computer applications, or any activity to further interests, cultivate reflective skills or broaden outlook is appropriate if without pressure. These students should not be forced, even subtly, into that exploration or study if they feel no need. The challenge here is to withstand the pressure from parents to force them into these activities. They need to enjoy a pressure-free childhood and youth. The logic of events in the years ahead will place enough demands upon them where they will be able to make valuable contributions to the world — in their time, in their way.

I have learned over many years in education that what is most needed for the gifted and the non-gifted is spiritual discernment, growth in the spiritual understanding that God is the source of all intelligence and capacity, that as offspring of God they and all others are the spiritual expression of God and therefore have the ability to express God's intelligence in whatever they are doing. This may be in intellectual pursuits, physical activities, artistic creations, business ventures or whatever they have to do. These things do not have to be great things as the world measures things – the reading of advanced literature, the solving of complex mathematical problems, the writing of soon to be forgotten essays. It can quite simply be enjoying the world around us, appreciating its beauty, running or hiking through its forests, crossing its mountains, streams, rivers and deserts, conversing with strangers, spending quiet moments with their own thoughts. Children and young people profit immeasurably from these kinds of activities because there is no hurry or anxiety about being better than or more advanced than others. The reading and writing and solving of problems comes naturally at their own rate of growth through the regular school curriculum.

This spiritual discernment brings with it great humility. Children learn from an early age not to set themselves above or below others for any reason. Neither do they do overlook the fact that some individuals run faster than others, some read with more understanding than others, some solve problems with more precision than others, some make wiser judgments than others. They also learn that those human facts do not prevent them and others from running faster later, reading more intelligently later, solving problems with precision later, making wise judgments later. They learn that growth through all avenues is safely left in God's hands, in God's time, in God's way.

This understanding does not prevent or interfere with efforts to excel, to perform at an optimum level. Those efforts should always be encouraged, but without intimidation by the fear of failure or anxiety if excellence is not forthcoming.

I am convinced that spiritual understanding is essential for all children and their growth in a balanced way through the school curriculum. Without it they are disadvantaged and too easily caught up in the clamour for haste and achievement that characterizes so much of the world scene. This is detrimental to the natural, full growth of children. It is not, however, the school's responsibility to provide instruction in that spiritual understanding. That belongs entirely to the home and church, mosque, synagogue or temple. The only responsibility of the school in this area is to maintain an atmosphere which supports the efforts of the home and religious bodies of all denominations to encourage their children to apply that understanding throughout the curriculum and in all school activities. That is not difficult to do as long as teachers, administrators and support staff are of outstanding character and consciously work for the elevation of character with every student.

Even a glimmer of spiritual understanding helps children and young people overcome the concern they may have about their speed of learning. They gradually learn to learn at a rate that is suitable for them. They come to realize that learning slowly today does not mean learning slowly tomorrow. And with increased understanding, the concept of slowness and quickness gives way to learning naturally at their own speed of expression, somewhat like a ray of light from the sun giving off the sun's light.

The only other area of the curriculum that needs to be addressed for character development is that of values. In character education the entire curriculum must be values-filled. Values, the ideals cherished by society that need to be furthered by each generation for the stability and progress of peoples, must appear in every part of the curriculum. The values furthered can be accepted by virtually all segments of society, regardless of religion, philosophy, belief. They need to be clearly identified and consistently promoted and upheld. I believe everyone in a democratic society would agree on the necessity for such values as honesty, integrity, openness, dignity, self-worth, respect, care, peace, goodwill, freedom and love. These values are all manifested and individualized in ways too numerous even to contemplate. In fact there is no limit to their manifestation.

Furtherance of these universal fundamental values precludes retaliation, revenge or recourse to violence to correct wrongs and injustices, perceived or real. Correction and adjustment are made through due process of laws, rules and regulations. All disputes are settled by appropriate grievance procedures, labour courts, negotiation, conciliation, mediation and arbitration. Children and young people learn early that there is no need for withdrawal of services or work stoppage at any time. And when they go out into the world, they will take those values to better the world for all. The key here, of course, is to ensure that teachers, administrators and support staff model the values being furthered — throughout the curriculum, the school and their own lives.

A business-oriented or economy-driven curriculum should never dominate public schools. Courses on business, labour, management, government, and other aspects of the economy may be offered, but they are peripheral to the academics, the arts and athletics. Public schools do not exist to prepare young people for specific jobs or positions or trades or professions. They prepare them for all markets and trades and professions by encouraging development of the educated citizen — the individual who is teachable, thoughtful, respectful, cooperative, principled, flexible, creative, imaginative, a thinker, problem-solver, producer.

Business, technology and service agencies can take these citizens and train them on the job themselves. That is their responsibility, not the responsibility of the school. Government assistance may have to be provided in some operations, but the school should never be used to replace that responsibility. And partnerships among business, labour, management, government and the school should never be established simply for career preparation. Vocational apprenticeships are best left to post High School. Nothing should be allowed to detract from the long-term character development that must go on within the world's great public schools.

Curricula related to Aboriginals, Blacks, Caucasians, Orientals, Metis, Incas, and specific ethnic groups can also be readily introduced. Courses and activities in these areas should not replace regular curriculum requirements. They can be offered through the Primary School, Middle School and High School where appropriate.

Countless racial, ethnic, language and religious groups demand of state and federal governments that separate schools be established and operated by government solely for their own group, with their own curriculum. I believe it is far better for their children and for society that they give up their special interests and have their children educated in the world's public non-sectarian education system. Parents and others can still preserve their own traditions, customs, religious views and practices by providing for them in the home, community, church, mosque, synagogue or temple. If their beliefs are strong enough and their children are taught to love and live them, even in the face of worldly pressure to abandon or compromise them, they should be strengthened in their use. If children and young people fail to do so, it illustrates either a weakness of teaching, a weakness of learning, or a weakness of character. All public schools can establish an atmosphere which enables children and young people to test the efficacy of their cultural, personal and religious beliefs and practices. That is done through the school's curriculum and focus on character development.

Should the curriculum include sex education, drug and alcohol education, tobacco education, gang education, health education, career education, life-styles education? It is impossible in a public education system not to deal with society's preoccupation with all these areas. The questions arise then as to *how, when* and *where* these areas can be addressed fairly and reasonably to meet the needs of children and young people, families and society, and at the same time accommodate wide diversity in family moral, spiritual, philosophical and personal beliefs and practices. In my view this is best accomplished by having knowledgeable school counsellors present factual information in each area, encourage students to examine the facts through the prism of the standards expected of the educated citizen, and then leave students and their parents to deal with the ways in which they wrestle with the magnetic pull toward permissive sex, drugs and alcohol, tobacco, gang involvement and dangerous life-styles. Matters of health, hygiene and personal problems are best left to counsellors and school health authorities to deal with on an individual basis. And information supplied here needs to be in keeping with family wishes. Sex education should be confined to its physical aspects, and birth control information provided without advice on its use. The moral, spiritual, emotional and social dimensions of sex should be left to the home and church, mosque, synagogue and temple, or any other community organization that families refer to for direction.

The school can begin with this part of the curriculum in Grade 6 and continue it until Grade 11. Provision must always be made for those parents who do not want to have their children taught by the school in any of these areas. The best way in this case is for the school to provide parents with the school's information — including videos, cassettes, software and printed material — and encourage them to give direction to their children at home, screened through their own beliefs and practices. Under all circumstances the school must respect the right of parents and their children to work out their own approach to the challenges of sex, drugs and alcohol, tobacco, and various life-styles. The effort of teachers, administrators and support staff to uphold high moral standards in their own lives will do more to promote healthy practices in children and young people than all their counsel and advice, however well meant.

Instruction in these areas should not be laboured and the amount of time spent should not be lengthy. It must not take away from the basic curriculum. One block of time in one semester in each of Grades 9, 10 and 11 is adequate in High School; one block of time for half of the school year in each of Grades 6, 7 and 8 is adequate in Middle School. There should also be little overlap of content from one grade to the next. As well, there should be a specific sequence in each of the areas examined, a sequence appropriate to the age level of the students being taught. While a state Ministry of Education should provide the basic content for all schools in its jurisdiction, schools should be free to make adjustments to the content and sequence to meet local needs.

There will always be strong individuals and special interest groups lobbying for curriculum additions. These range from the mundane to the esoteric, from marriage education to theology. Most need to be rejected. If some demands are reasonable and satisfy specified criteria established by teachers, administrators and parents, courses can be offered as electives at the High School level. Nothing, however, must take away from the basic curriculum.

There is one curriculum-related programme that needs careful monitoring to ensure everything within it is furthering character development. This is the extra- or co-curricular programme, so-called as it supplements or complements the basic curriculum. It is an extremely important programme for all students. For many children and young people it has as much or more influence in shaping their individuality as does the basic curriculum. It is imperative therefore that all activities within that programme — the arts, athletics, theatre, student government, clubs — be conducted with the fashioning of character in mind.

Several things must be in place here for appropriate development to take place. First, there must be emphasis on high level performance in almost all activities. The activities are not for frivolity or for leisurely pursuit. Strong demands are needed for growth in staying power, singleness of purpose, obedience to rules and regulations, unselfishness, peak performance. The high level of performance helps break down beliefs of limited ability and encourages others to go beyond the levels others have demonstrated.

The danger here is to avoid build-up of self, the second essential. Singling out children and young people for outstanding performance can be damaging. The recognition often leads to self-centredness, which in turn inhibits overall development. Media publicity is particularly damaging in this regard. Many children and young people spend years, and some a lifetime, working out of that thought-on-self, a vexing constriction to growth.

Third, children and young people should remain within their chronological age group for almost all activities. This is to help guard against individuals being forced into situations they are not ready to handle emotionally, socially, physically, psychologically, morally or spiritually. So many children and young people, seemingly more mature than others of their own age and possessing talents and abilities far beyond others of their age, give the appearance that they are ready to deal with others of similar ability. The fact is they are not. A sound rule to establish is to have children take part in almost all activities only with those of their own chronological age — born within the same calendar year. Exceptions are inevitable, but they should be rare, such as when various age groups must come together for an entire school production or in isolated communities where numbers in each year are small.

Fourth, only teachers, administrators and some support staff, those thoroughly versed in character development, should conduct, coach or direct extra-curricular activities. There are many well-meaning parents and community members longing to do so and who appear to be good models to emulate. But they should not be permitted to do so. The reason is that there is no control and no assurance that they are conducting the activities in keeping with the high standards established by those professionally trained. Short courses on character education for parents and others are insufficient to guarantee that they themselves are of the character desired. I have seen great damage done to young people by superficially good volunteer coaches, sponsors and mentors. They were well-meaning, intelligent, and ignorant. It has to be the rule and practice that only those involved in the day to day character education of children and young people conduct the extra-curricular programmes for the school. It follows that all teachers and administrators must take part in these activities and be responsible for them.

Under no circumstance should an extra-curricular programme, either within-school or between-schools, begin before the first year of Middle School (Grade 6). Middle School programmes should not pattern those of the High School, especially those of a highly competitive nature, such as athletics. Children need to remain children as long as possible. Patterning young people and their activities does not lend itself to that and works against the natural development of individuality. This does not mean there should be no inter-school competition in the Middle School. It means that emphasis on competition in terms of recognition, awards and championships should be significantly less than in High School.

It is essential to remember throughout the curriculum — basic and extra-curricular — that the curriculum is simply the avenue for development of character. Serious losses occur in that development if focus on the primary purpose of education is blurred and emphasis is placed on performance and the acquisition of skills and knowledge for their own sake. Abilities, skills and knowledge are to be taken out into the world and made practical by thoughtful, respectful, cooperative and principled young people. That aim within the curriculum must never be lost sight of by the school and society.

Chapter 5

Individualized Teaching

One universal basic curriculum is essential for every school throughout the world. How that curriculum is taught or presented by teachers is an individual demonstration. Each teacher must work out over a number of years of experience the methods he or she is comfortable and effective with. Experience shows me that this working out takes at least ten years of conscientious teaching. Teaching effectiveness is determined by student achievement, performance, knowledge, skills and character development in terms of the educated citizen. Effectiveness cannot be determined simply by student achievement, performance, knowledge and skills. It is character that determines the use of those abilities, so abilities and character have to be connected. While the student is ultimately responsible for that development, there must be concentration on that development by the teacher in everything taught.

Much is said about children's learning styles and how teachers must provide for the wide variation in ways in which children learn. There is some truth to those observations, and teachers may need to experiment with various methods for different students on many occasions. Those methods may include emphasis on use of the physical senses — taste, touch, sight, sound, smell; reliance on personal experience, on reason, on intuition, on authoritative views, on any other approach teachers have cultivated through experience or training. The important point to remember in these approaches is, however, that each teacher must decide what is appropriate in encouraging children and young people to learn and grow in development of their capacities.

It is also important that children themselves adapt to the different teaching methods of their teachers. Children have many teachers over the Primary, Middle School and High School years. And beyond that, throughout life, they will be working with hundreds of individuals who have widely differing approaches to learning. Children need to learn early to learn from each teacher whatever they can and not complain about teachers and their methods of teaching. Great character growth occurs as children learn to do this, especially in terms of flexibility, openness of thought, inventiveness and originality. A highly critical thought is gradually replaced with a non-critical, mild thought, receptive to the new and fresh. The complaining, petty intellect, found even among children, gives way to a freer, more grateful-for-the-good, thought. This in no way lessens the analytical abilities of children. Quite the contrary results: children learn to look for the good in each situation and become highly perceptive of both the desirable and the undesirable, in academics and in other areas.

So whether to use recitation, choral-work, drill, memory, question and answer, discussion, debate, explanation, demonstration, experiment, observation, analysis, lecturing, hands-on use of technology, listening, viewing, mentoring, tutoring, team teaching, student-partner teaching, or whatever other method seems appropriate to the age and development of children and young people, is a decision to be made only by each teacher. That professional autonomy must always be protected by the school, by school boards, and by state ministries of education.

Where teachers fail to be effective in their methods of instruction in the context of development of the whole child, they should most definitely be removed from teaching and their teaching certificates revoked permanently. That should be done only after a full school year's effort has been made to assist the teacher to be effective. The assistance should be provided by no fewer than two of the teacher's teaching colleagues from the same level — Primary, Middle School or High School. School and district administrators should not be involved in the assistance provided nor in the evaluation at the end of that school year. At least two other teachers from the appropriate level should do the evaluation. That evaluation must consider effectiveness again from the total development of children and include all school activities in which the teacher has been involved with children and adults. The basic questions to be answered by the evaluators are these: Has the teacher had a significant impact upon the progress of his or her students in terms of achievement, performance, knowledge, skills, thoughtfulness, respectfulness, cooperation, principled behaviour, flexibility, originality, problem-solving, thinking, producing? Has the teacher contributed to the overall development of children or young people in this school? Has he or she been a model of the educated citizen the school is striving to graduate? If there is no reasonable doubt, the teacher should be absolved of all doubt. If there is reasonable doubt, the teacher should be required to leave at the end of that school year and the state licensing authority be asked to take away the individual's teaching certificate.

The purpose of teaching is to awaken students to the potential for good they all possess. That potential can be realized only as they grow in knowledge, skills and character. It is the job of the teacher to help students in that growth. Part of that job includes awakening the student to the level of insight and understanding and skill of the teacher, be that in academics, the arts, athletics or career preparation. To do that the teacher must exhibit and teach about that understanding and insight and skill. The teacher must demonstrate or have demonstrated the skills to be learned. The teacher must take each student and lead him or her from the present level to a higher level. The teacher can never be therefore simply a facilitator or leader or motivator or guide, someone setting the stage for children to learn on their own. The teacher is always an awakener, a teacher, and must therefore teach. That is very hard work. A youth leader may take youth on a hike, a trip to see the beauties of the mountains, and youth may bask in those beauties and benefit from the hike. But that is not teaching. That is only leading, guiding, motivating, facilitating.

Teaching is extremely difficult. It demands more thought, energy, patience, insight, inspiration and affection than virtually any other human activity. It is a never-ending effort to awaken the receptive or unreceptive thought to its unlimited potential in the use of human capacities. The same affection and attention must be given to both the receptive and the unreceptive. The teacher never knows when thought and feeling awaken to the teaching. Children and young people awaken when least expected. The teacher must always be ready therefore to nourish them when they do awake. And that nourishment is basically more attention, more affection, more encouragement.

The conscientious teacher's work is therefore never done. It is for this reason that teachers need ample time for rest and renewal. And it is only the conscientious, those who understand and appreciate that they fashion nations and the world and are willing to devote themselves to that fashioning, who should teach children and young people.

Teaching, then, is the principal activity going on within every school. It is individualized by each teacher in his or her own way. No one should interfere with that individualization. It is a fact that where there is teaching, there is learning; where there is little or no teaching, simply talking about it, simply facilitating or arranging for learning, there is little or no learning. And the little learning may well be incidental, lacking specific direction and purpose. Students cannot be expected to learn on their own without clear direction with regard to what they are supposed to be learning. So even if there are first-rate buildings, facilities, resources, technology, administrators and support personnel, unless there is an emphasis on teaching, learning will be minimal and children and young people will benefit only slightly from school. And most noticeable will be their lack of character development. That should never be allowed. But if it does exist, steps must be taken immediately to shift the school's focus back to teaching and the teacher's right to individualize that teaching with concentration on character development.

Chapter 6

Rotation in Administration

In order to establish and maintain a focus on character education within the world's public schools a major shift must be made in the current relationship between administration and teaching. At the moment administration dominates public education at both school and district level. It does this by maintaining a self-perpetuating hierarchy of district administrators, school administrators, teachers and support staff in a descending order of perceived importance, control and influence over the education of children. Its misplaced importance has evolved over many years as a result of administrators' delusions of self-importance and the subtle but hardening acceptance of that view by teachers, parents and public. Administration has become one of the unknown gods educators and society ignorantly worship. Self-fulfilling belief has fashioned the perception that the key component to successful schools and school districts is the administrative team. At the school level this is the principal, vice-principals and administrative assistants; at the district level it is the superintendent of schools or director of education, the secretary-treasurer or comptroller, and the district's management team of assistant or associate superintendents, directors of instruction and directors of various operations including personnel, employee relations, maintenance, operations, purchasing and business — depending upon the size of the district.

Administrators and education researchers claim that successful schools and school districts have at their helms administrators who give visionary educational leadership to programmes and activities. Research continues to support this view simply because if schools and districts are not accredited or recognized as being successful, administrators are replaced until they carry out what more senior administrators identify for school boards as being successful. This is not leadership. It is implementation — implementation of what others dictate or determine. My experience is that administrators are neither visionary nor educational leaders. (In the thirty-something years I laboured in this field, I met only one administrator I could call an educational leader. And he was not visionary. He knew clearly what was needed for children in terms of character and values and carried out everything for his school board that enabled teachers to fashion that character. All organizational and administrative recommendations and decisions were made from that standpoint. He was basically a teacher who ensured that administration served the teacher.)

Administrators are actually managers, coordinators, organizers, delegators, motivators, doers. In education they are essentially teachers who are taking time out from teaching to serve other teachers. Whether at the school level or at the district level they are corporate officers who must carry out the directives of school boards and ministries of education. They advise and recommend to these bodies and then they carry out or implement whatever these bodies decide. They work closely with teachers, students, parents and community groups. They inform, consult, advise, coordinate, direct and organize. They do this for the most part with great sensitivity and cooperation, but this does not qualify them as leaders in education. If they do their job as it should be done, they serve in fact as servants – servants to the system, to the public, to other administrators, to parents, to teachers, to students. The individuals they must always serve most directly are the teachers, who in turn fashion the character of their students.

That, however, is not what school and district administrators believe they are. They see themselves as leaders of teachers – of supervision and evaluation of instruction, of professional development, of curriculum implementation, of programme evaluation, of public relations, of the direction in which education should be moving. All administrators give recognition to the importance of teaching, claiming that they themselves love teaching, but few ever return to teach on a full-time basis. Administrators have in effect placed themselves above teaching. That is where the hierarchy started — in the minds of administrators. And practices of self-promotion, self-selection, self-perpetuation have cemented the hierarchy so that a true educational leader within the teaching profession, someone doing the thinking for the ages in terms of freeing children and society, someone wishing to broaden experience in the field, would have great difficulty getting an opportunity to gain administrative experience. The hierarchical thought has separated administrators from their colleagues and disqualified them from being educational leaders or people with vision. The individual with vision has to be completely un-selfed. The present system does not allow for that to surface. It forces individuals to concentrate on self for their own security and progress.

The myth that administrators are the educational leaders in schools and school districts has been reinforced by practices which encourage teachers to leave teaching and move permanently into administration. These include inflated salaries, opportunities for further administrative promotions, more power in the positions, and more status in the eyes of themselves and popular thought. The myth has also been perpetuated by ministries of education, made up primarily of former school and district administrators, by school boards, made up of sincere but naive board members, and by the public, not really aware of what takes place within the public school system.

This emphasis on administration and its mythical nature as a leadership position, the steady flow of teachers out of teaching into administration as a permanent career, the payment of exorbitant salaries for administrators, and the lack of recognition of the value of teachers, needs to be halted. Then a reversal of importance between teaching and administration can be made. I believe the immediate solution is rotation in administration and a change in salary scales. With rotation, all teachers who qualify — those who are principled, efficient, well-organized, cooperative, energetic, experienced (with at least ten years of successful teaching experience), knowledgeable and dedicated to the elevation of character — can serve as administrators for a few years and then return to teaching. These individuals can readily serve as assistant principals for four to five years and then serve as principals for another four to five years. They should then return to teaching permanently. Under no condition should teachers serve more than a total of ten years in these positions in their careers. And under no condition should any individual serve more than ten years in administration without returning to a full-time teaching position.

Those wishing to serve as school district administrators should apply only after having served as a school administrator and only after returning to a teaching position. School district administrators should never be appointed from school administrative positions. Appointment of administrators solely from teaching will help emphasize the importance of teaching. All district administrative appointments should be for limited terms. There should be no more than two three-year appointments for any position except that of superintendent of schools or chief executive officer. In that position a maximum of two four-year appointments should be ensured. In all cases individuals in these positions should return to a teaching position permanently. They should not serve again in district or school administrative positions.

Selection and appointment of all administrators — school and district — should be done by school board members themselves. Board members should conduct the short-listing and interviews, with the assistance of the superintendent or designate, a teacher representative and a parent representative. It is essential that there be no control of appointments by the superintendent or any other administrator. It is imperative that all qualified teachers demonstrating administrative proclivities and a desire to serve as an administrator be given the opportunity to serve. No personal, political, gender, ethnic, racial or religious differences should interfere with this opportunity. The willingness and ability to work for character development in all children must be the chief determinant in appointments.

All school administrative appointments should be made whenever possible at least eight months in advance of a new school year. This allows for appropriate transfer and placement of teachers and support staff in an orderly way.

Salaries for all administrators, including district administrators, must not be higher than for the highest paid teacher. Hours of work, workload, complexity of decisions, demands upon patience, knowledge of systems, and relationships with others are of no more importance in the world's public school system than is the education of a nation's children carried on daily by conscientious teachers.

Rotation in administration will be resisted world-wide because it will destroy the present hierarchy. It will do away with pride of power, position and prestige in administration, and many in these positions will lose their control over others and the education of children. As well, those aspiring for power, position and prestige will not be able to look forward to that on a permanent basis.

Nevertheless, a bold move needs to be made in this area. This one single revolutionary move will bring great freedom to the world's public education system and place accountability and importance in education where they rightfully belong — on the teacher, who in turn is freed to free his or her students. Freedom from oppression, freedom from suppression, freedom of expression, freedom of opportunity, freedom to satisfy aspirations, are inherent here for all teachers. The world's children will be the real beneficiaries as they become the focus of the increased freedom of their teachers. Then character development will truly flourish.

Chapter 7

Parent Obligations and Involvement

To advance character education throughout the world parent obligations and parent involvement in school functions and activities need to be clearly identified. The need is imperative because what has happened over the years has been an eroding through societal pressures of fulfilling parent responsibilities, and efforts by some parents to dictate what public schools should be doing. This is particularly pervasive in the more advanced technological countries where virtually all parents have received relatively high levels of education and thereby consider themselves authoritative about education.

The fact is, however, that mere attendance at school does not make an individual an authority on education. And it does not qualify anyone to have insight on how best to educate children. That insight comes only from hard-earned experience in the front-line of teaching. And even with that experience, unless there has been a focus on the essentials of education — elevation of the mind and heart of every student — one may not become authoritative. I recall teaching and coaching a number of students and later giving them the opportunity to teach and coach others. They taught the knowledge and skills but failed to help students unleash their potential simply because they had not grasped the spirit of the teachings. The same applies to parents educated in the public schools. They have been through the system, but may well have failed to grasp the spirit, the real purpose of the system – to awaken children to their potential.

It is therefore only the teachers and administrators working daily within the system who know what children need from an educational standpoint. Parents should not then get involved in the education of their children other than to support teachers in their professional efforts. This support should be minimal. It should include only the following areas: support the school's efforts to educate the whole child; serve in a consultative capacity only; freely and openly offer opinions on school issues when sought; respect and accept the professional judgment of teachers and administrators; supervise and chaperone on field trips and excursions; fund-raise when needed; assist in the organization and running of events such as book days, sports days, graduation ceremonies.

It is dangerous for parents to be involved in much more than this within schools. Many would like to become involved in helping children develop skills in academic and practical areas of the curriculum, in selecting personnel, in determining curriculum and school practices, in evaluating individual teaching methods, in controlling school meetings, in coaching athletes, debating teams or drama students. These are professional areas best left to the total direction of teachers. The potential for parent interference in the character development of children as carried on by the school is large. That is why parents should discipline themselves to take or send their children to school and leave them there alone with their teachers.

For the sake of children and their character development parents should confine themselves to these few areas of involvement and concentrate on fulfilling a few essential obligations that only a parent can fulfil. These are basically to ensure children go to school every day ready to learn. That includes sending children to school well fed, fully rested, cleanly dressed, studies completed, encouraged to look for the good in every teacher and activity, encouraged to take part willingly in school activities, encouraged to value the school and its role in helping the home to educate them. It also includes refraining from criticism of teachers and the school. This is not to ignore real problems of the school. Those should be met openly and directly by parents and the school. But that can be done privately without embroiling children. Where these few obligations are met by parents, their children will benefit immeasurably. They will attend school daily, prepared to be receptive to the teachings of their teachers — ripe for growth in character.

Where children do not have the benefit of conscientious parents to prepare them properly for school, social agencies, in cooperation with the school, may well have to step in and assist with this preparation. That may include the feeding, clothing, washing, resting and encouraging that all children must have. The school must not have that preparation placed upon it. The school has the major task that no other agency can successfully undertake — the development of character — and must confine itself to that task. Other social agencies such as health and welfare must assume responsibilities in this area of sending children to school ready to learn.

The public needs reminding periodically that teachers teach, children learn, and parents prepare their children to learn. And where parents fail to fulfil their obligations, someone else has to assume those obligations. The main reason for lack of growth on the part of children is parental neglect. That has nothing to do with the economic or social standing of parents. It has everything to do with insufficient love of the children and an all-absorbing self-love. Parents can do nothing greater for the world than properly prepare their children for school. They do not have to teach, they do not have to learn, they simply have to provide for and prepare their children for that learning. An unselfish love, a stable marriage, even in the midst of dire circumstances, will work wonders for those children.

Lack of food, clothing and shelter by parents who cannot possibly provide them for their children is not parental neglect. Where these conditions exist, state governments need to provide these basic essentials so parents can supply the love needed and help prepare their children for the learning that is as essential as the basic human needs of safety, shelter and nourishment.

So parent obligations are few but essential in preparing children to learn and to develop fully. And parent involvement in schools must be minimal to allow for teachers to concentrate on their major task of character development.

Chapter 8

Funding

In order to bring about the character development essential for individual, community and world progress, adequate funds must be provided for public education. These funds should be funnelled through one major channel within every state, province or jurisdictional region. This should be the state government governing each defined area within a country. While the federal or national government within a country should provide education funds for special circumstances, those funds should be given only to state governments so that they in turn can allocate those funds as the state determines. States must guarantee full use and appropriate allocation of those federal funds.

Federal governments should not be involved in the governance of education under any circumstances. They can and should be involved in collecting funds, but should not determine or influence how those funds should be spent. Their primary purpose in supplying funds is to help ensure equity in education throughout a country. Some regions of a country, for example, may not have the economic or personal income base to support public education as well as other regions. It should be the job of the federal government in those cases to supply the funds comparable to those of the more financially well-off states. This practice is not a competition for federal funds; it is a practice to bring relative equity in public education to a country.

Specific areas for which federal funding may be required are directly related to federal initiatives such as immigration, language training, job training, skills up-grading, cultural and heritage preservation, national assessment, equality of opportunity, sexual equality, religious equality, political equality, judicial equality. The addressing of these federal issues through public education must be left to local or state governments.

While federal governments may raise funds for public education through income tax, sales tax, value-added tax, service tax, or any other system which the people deem appropriate, the main system of funding for public education should be conducted by state governments. They should gather the needed funds through personal income tax, commercial property tax, residential property tax, sales tax and an education tax. Every citizen within a state should contribute financially to the public education of its children. This can best be done by state governments collecting through income tax returns 1% of net income from every citizen within the state. That tax, an education tax, must be used only for public education. All must pay this tax, including those who have no children and those who choose to send their children to private, parochial, denominational, dissentient, independent or separate schools. All citizens are beneficiaries of the public schools; not all citizens are beneficiaries of private, parochial, denominational, dissentient, independent or separate schools, just as all citizens are not beneficiaries of Sunday Schools. It is primarily those who subscribe to their religious, philosophical or personal beliefs.

Neither state nor federal funds gathered from these sources and by these means should be provided to any private, parochial, denominational, dissentient, independent or separate school. The public has no jurisdiction, control or influence over those schools and therefore no funds should be provided for them. Every one of these schools exists to further its own religion, philosophy or way of life, and so it should, but financed only by those who wish to further those ideas and practices. Once any one of these schools accepts public funds the state government should immediately appoint members of the public to sit on its board of governors to direct the public interest in the use of those funds. The number of government-appointed members should coincide with the percentage of its operating funds coming from the public purse.

For those parents and others who have intense desires to send their children to non-public schools for a variety of reasons, arrangements can be made through municipal governments — cities, towns, villages — to have their personal residential property taxes sent directly to the school of their choosing. Those taxes do not go to the state government and are thereby not taken out of the public purse for financing of non-public schools. As well, deductions on personal income tax can be arranged for funds expended by parents for their children attending non-public schools. This again is not public funding of these schools. The same privilege should be extended to parents providing funds for public education for their children. These cases are rare but they may occur where funds have been submitted to public schools as donations or fund-raising monies. These arrangements bring a measure of financial fairness to those intent on supporting non-public schools and at the same time ensure that public funds are not used to finance private, parochial, denominational, dissentient, independent or separate schools. They remain totally self-supporting.

Arguments that non-public schools save the public money are specious. The public schools can readily accommodate all children enrolled in these schools and funding will readily be supplied by the public for their education in the public system. If parents and others do not wish to send their children to public schools that is indeed their right. But it must not be at public expense.

State legislation should be in place to ensure that local boards of public education cannot do their own taxing or fund-raising for capital and operating costs. State and federal governments alone must be the fund-raisers. And the state government should ensure an equality of financing and educational quality throughout the state. Local taxation and fund-raising through referendum or petition or direct taxation only works to produce an inequality in funds, services and programmes. And if private companies, large or small, wish to provide funds for schools, that should be done by giving those funds to the state. The state will then allocate those on an equitable basis where the need is greatest. Otherwise schools with business bases and those with aggressive fund-raisers bring an imbalance to regions, districts and schools. All schools must have the best in terms of buildings, facilities and equipment. Isolated areas of a state have children who need the same opportunity for character development as do urban and suburban children.

How much money is to be collected from the people and how much is to be spent on public education is a matter to be worked out according to regional conditions. This will vary widely depending upon the availability of monies, which depends greatly upon global, national and state economies. A reasonable guide is to set aside 25% of state revenue for public school education. This would include capital, operating, and debt reduction expenditures. This would also be apart from monies set aside for post-High School education.

The percentage of federal revenue for public education to be channelled to states would depend greatly upon the policies in effect from year to year at the federal level. Wide ranges in percentage could be expected here, depending also upon the stage of development of each country. Those still in the developing stages may well have to allow for greater percentages for public education than more highly developed countries.

While the tendency will be to compare one country with another in terms of revenues, expenditures and salaries, this should be avoided. It is never a question of monies with regard to quality of character development. It is always a question of quality of teachers dedicated to the task of character education regardless of funds or lack of funds. All the money in the world will not supply that quality. As the world comes to value that quality it will be willing to pay handsomely for it. It must first recognize it to see it. The onus on state governments and local school boards therefore is always to ensure outstanding character in a nation's teaching force. First rate salaries for teachers and first rate working conditions according to state and national standards are imperative. Then appropriate financing of buildings, facilities, equipment and resources can follow over time.

Provision must also be made for continual renewal, renovation and replacement of all buildings, facilities and equipment. This is a never-ending task. Modernization and up-dating are important for all schools and districts. This encourages children themselves to keep abreast of the times and keep thought focused on the new and contemporary. This is a vital part of their character development.

Chapter 9

Politics and Religion

Two of the greatest dangers to public education and its role in the development of the educated citizen are politics and religion. It is essential that everyone involved in and supportive of its efforts to educate the world's children understands the dangers and protects the system against these adverse influences. Both politics and religion operate subtly to infiltrate public education and control the education of children. Their influence is detrimental to the children's development because they both produce on-going monolithic, hierarchical, dominant, oppressive practices. Children become submissive to the system, and, except for those who innately do their own thinking, unknowingly perpetuate the hierarchical system. The result is stifled thought: there is an inability to openly question, to openly discuss, to openly debate, to openly dialogue; there is no challenge to authority, to established practice; there is, in sum, an inability to play an effective role in a truly democratic society — a society characterized by government at all levels which furthers rule of the majority with respect and protection of the rights of the minority, government that fosters widely diverse views and practices, government, in the words of Abraham Lincoln, "of the people, by the people, for the people."

Of the two dangers to public education and the total development of children, the greater danger is religion. The religion referred to here is monolithic religion. Monolithic religions are religions dominated by a clergy who insist, openly or subtly, that their beliefs, practices and

53

followers rule and occupy virtually all positions of influence and power within a nation. These religions, if not checked by the people, result in church states and state churches. They do not allow for the free exercise of secular institutions and practices as that lessens their power and dominance.

The major problem with monolithic religion is that only those who subscribe to its beliefs and practices have freedom of thought, conscience and activity. Supposedly only these individuals are the chosen of God. Those who do not subscribe to these beliefs and practices are deprived of their freedom by being excluded from opportunities for growth and progress. They become lesser citizens, silent slaves to the dominant thought. In education they have a place within the hierarchy of the system, but it is always a place where they can be directed, controlled and influenced — always subservient to those in positions of greater power and influence. They are quite unknowingly the victims of oppression, suppression and repression. And the ultimate sufferers of this domination are the children. The system perpetuates itself and few children can come out of such a restrictive education system as free, creative or imaginative thinkers.

To ensure freedom for a nation's people and the sound education of their children, church and state must remain forever separate, and religious liberty for all guaranteed in constitutions, courts and human affairs. All religions, from the bizarre to the common, from the smallest to the largest, must be allowed, within the bounds of law and reasonableness, to rise or fall on their own merits. The inexorable march of time and education of the populace will determine length of existence and effectiveness of each distinct religion.

Ironically, religion in its best form offers the world, and education in particular, its greatest promise. It can provide the world with the finest education system possible, a system that allows for all children, regardless of religious or non-religious background, to develop their potential. Religion at its best speaks to the people about the divine; it does not speak about the human scene. It explains to human consciousness what constitutes the divine, what God is, and how God and God's ideas govern the divine, including the spiritual man of God's creating. As men, women and children come to understand and appreciate this spiritual sense of things, the human begins to pattern the divine and there appears in civil, religious, political, educational, economic, judicial and legislative matters greater peace, good will, law, order, and care for all and the universe. Oppression, suppression and repression dissolve in time. All individuals are left alone to work out their own destiny and place in the human scene — alone with God and conscience.

This type of religious thought is the basis for all human progress. It results in true democracy. So where theocracy now exists, it will ultimately have to be replaced with democracy. Where neither theocracy nor democracy exists, people in those regions should grow gradually directly into democracy and avoid the suffering of passing through a theocracy and generations later into a democracy. All their institutions need to be run on a democratic basis. This must include provision for universal public education, which is essentially universal character development.

The watching that needs to take place in public education with regard to religion, then, is to ensure no domination of the public system by any religion. This watch must go on day and night. Unless guarded against, religious domination can occur over-night and very subtly through the appointment of teachers, administrators and support staff with overwhelming numbers from a particular religion. This is particularly true in positions of authority and influence. It can occur with governments, school boards and management consultants doing the recommending or appointing. Governments and school boards therefore need to ensure diversity of religion in the appointment of teachers, administrators and support staff. Personnel departments need to be directed to guarantee this diversity. Appointments of individuals to oversee this diversity are the key appointments within the public system. Integrity must be the hallmark of the individuals selected.

Public schools must also be free of being used by religious groups to further their denominational teachings. No religious literature of a denominational nature should be distributed by the schools and no denominational or devotional exercises should be offered by the schools. This does not include courses on religion, which should be an essential part of the High School elective programme. Numerous courses on religion at this level are desirable to foster understanding and appreciation of the thinking and practices of those who follow different religions.

Growth in character for all children occurs best in a truly secular public school setting. The reason is that children learn that all, regardless of religious background or lack of religious background, are the same — truly offspring of the same divine Parent, commonly called God. All are equal in the eyes of God and all are equal in the eyes of one another, all working for the common good of one another. There should be no thought of who should be the greatest, whose religion is right or the nearest right.

The truly public secular school system actually has more spirituality permeating its system than any religious school because it allows for the development of every child, free from indoctrination from any specific denominational belief, free from the belief that some children are better than others, and free to practise within the school the beliefs taught by the child's home and church, mosque, temple or synagogue. The public school becomes the testing ground for those religious beliefs. Children learn to cross swords with beliefs contrary to those taught at home and in church, mosque, temple or synagogue. It is imperative for the preservation of that spirituality, therefore, that no religion dominate in the world's public education system, a system dedicated to the development of every child.

Politics is also a serious threat to public universal character education. It is not quite the danger that religion is because its presence is more readily detected and more easily checked. Nevertheless it is a danger and must be nullified, if not eliminated. The politics referred to here is that carried on by bona fide political bodies with specific platforms on educational reforms. Well-meaning and not so well-meaning political bodies may set out to change public education to fit in with their social, economic and military views. The schools in their view should become the agents for change in these areas. This may include involving children in peace marches, banning of arms, raising money for the poor and homeless, furthering family planning, birth control or abortion, or saving the planet from pollution. It may also include efforts to further privatization, entrepreneurism, capitalism, communism, socialism or totalitarianism. These efforts need to be stopped before they get into the schools. Public schools are not avenues for the furtherance of particular political views. All views can be examined objectively without being furthered.

The danger with politics in public education is that political parties can take over that education through local school boards and use the schools to further their political philosophies. Public schools must always remain politically neutral. They exist to elevate character. That is above and beyond politics. Political parties of any type — communist, socialist, capitalist — should be excluded by law from taking over the public education system.

The best way to keep public education free from both politics and religion is to have all school board members appointed by the state government. The dangers here are that the government will appoint only those who subscribe to its political views and that with every change of government there will be a corresponding change in personalities on school boards. Also distasteful to many is that local citizens will not have the opportunity to elect those they wish to have represent them and thereby have a less democratic system of government locally. These arguments are valid, but the need to eliminate politics and religion from public education and to ensure high standards in the appointment of all within the public education system outweighs these considerations. I believe these appointments, if undertaken seriously and with great care, so that appointees are not government clones and have wide diversity in political and religious backgrounds, will ensure that.

Election of school board members results in too wide a disparity in quality of members. Diversity among school board members enriches, disparity destroys. This disparity ranges from the sublime to the ludicrous in motives, morals, abilities, appreciation and understanding of public education. Public education has suffered seriously from this disparity with those within the system unable to focus on the essential purpose of education — the awakening of children to their potential for good. So a major change must be made in the selection of those governing local school boards, from elected to appointed.

These appointed members must then become responsible for the selection and appointment of all employees within their jurisdiction. This will ensure the high standards needed by all within the system to promote the development of character so necessary for all the world's children.

Chapter 10

Ethics

Ethics in education is just as important as ethics in every other avenue of life. In fact, ethics is probably more important here because it is in education that children early learn what is right and what is wrong. They learn this through their studies, their play, their student government, their contact with hundreds of others. Most of all they learn this from their teachers.

Ethics refers to standards of conduct, to the moral principles by which individuals are guided. There is no human activity not touched by ethics. It is important therefore for children to learn what is appropriate and what is inappropriate in their activities.

Teachers teach ethics by precept and example. They must therefore know themselves what is right and what is wrong in situations and must practise consciously and unconsciously whatever is right. Consistency in this practice is essential for children. There are hundreds of situations teachers meet daily calling for ethical and moral judgment. These include challenges of plagiarism, cheating on assignments and examinations, stealing, lying, self-righteousness, condemnation, complaining about others and conditions, breaking of confidences and promises, retaliation, revenge, hatred, jealousy, and personality conflicts. There is in fact little time in a day when teachers do not have ethical and moral decisions to make. So all teachers, whether or not they wish to be, are fashioners of morals and ethics in children and young people.

The teacher's example is certainly a strong fashioner of children's morals and ethics. But it must be accompanied with precept. Children, and even young people, need to be told what is right and what is wrong. Some need little or no explanation. They may have been taught what is right and what is wrong by their parents and their church, mosque, synagogue or temple. Others may have been taught virtually nothing. They need considerable direction and explanation of why some things are appropriate and other things are inappropriate. This is a major burden for teachers. The demand is incessant, never-ending. Coupled with the discipline that must necessarily accompany inappropriate responses to ethical situations, such as cheating, lying, stealing, reacting to direction, this makes a teacher's load heavy. And it becomes heavier or lighter depending upon the development and receptivity of the children or young people taught. It is not so much the number of children that makes for the burden as it is the level of moral development and the receptivity to the teacher's direction.

High ethical standards are essential for proper character education. They determine in large measure the degree to which students become thoughtful, respectful, cooperative, principled; they ultimately determine their degree of flexibility, creativity, originality, inventiveness; they also determine the level to which children and young people develop their ability to think, to solve problems, to produce, to perform.

The relationship between ethics, morals and performance is one that is little understood. It is in fact tied in closely to the development of individual potential. I came across this relationship in my mid-teens when I discovered to my dismay that my performance on the sports field coincided with my ethics and morals. If I lied to someone, cheated on a test, or was not completely honest, my performance on the basketball court, baseball diamond or track was poor and unpredictable, whereas if I lived in harmony with what I had been taught at home, church and school, the performance was predictably good. Inconsistency in applying what I had discovered prevented me from using the insight appropriately. Many years later, when coaching high school and college teams, I observed the same phenomenon with many of the players. I tried to explain the phenomenon to some of them, but they had difficulty grasping the relationship between morals and performance. I did not pursue the explanation as I felt there was not the receptivity needed to make the knowledge practical to them. But there is a definite cause and effect relationship here that relates to character development and the development of individual potential. It needs to be examined more deeply for the benefit of the individual, society, and the world.

Ethical and moral standards have to be addressed therefore by every teacher, administrator and support person in public education. They cannot be ignored or treated lightly. It follows that every individual involved with the public school system designed to elevate character must possess high ethical and moral standards. This includes school board members, district administrators, school administrators, support staff, volunteers and teachers. This will help maintain a high level of ethics and morals for the system and for the children and young people.

Standards such as those identified here have been furthered by many societies over the generations. They need to have even wider acceptance by the generations of today and tomorrow. Wording like the following could be used to state clearly the standards expected of all within the system.

This school district encourages its employees and appointed officials to maintain high standards in all dealings with each other and in carrying out tasks. These standards include adherence to honesty, openness, forthrightness, friendliness, fairness, equality, sensitivity to feelings, freedom of expression, allowance for differences in points of view, and respect for all.

This public education system exists to elevate students, to encourage all students to work towards fulfilment of their potential, and thereby to make a contribution to the world. All within the system need consciously to support that purpose. That is best done by maintaining high standards in dealings with everyone.

Chapter 11

Summary and Legislative Guide

It should be clearly apparent from this book that there are specific basic elements that must be in place both to establish and to maintain a public education system that fosters universal character education. These include one philosophy, one basic curriculum, one standard for teachers, one standard for students, autonomy in teaching, rotation in administration, specific parent support, adequate funding, political and religious absence, and high ethical and moral standards. Once these are in place they need to be maintained indefinitely. This is done by yearly renewal. All working within the system should review two of the elements every year so that over five years every aspect has been refocused. This will ensure on-going renewal and sharpness.

To incorporate these elements in law and to guarantee sound development of the world's children through public universal character education, state legislatures throughout the world need to pass appropriate laws and regulations governing public education. In developed countries these may well have to replace current laws and regulations. In less developed countries they may need to be the initial laws and regulations. The laws and regulations need to cover only the areas identified here and a few others not identified. These few other areas are important but have not been dealt with here because they are not essential elements of character development. These latter areas deal with services such as transportation, accommodation, buildings and grounds. Set forth in the following pages are guides to establishment of these laws and regulations. They are not intended to be exhaustive, simply legislative guides.

Article 1 — Foundation

SECTION 1: *PHILOSOPHY*. The philosophy for all public education within a state must be universal. That is, it must be the same for every public school. A philosophy does not vary with local conditions or the idiosyncrasies of diverse populations. It is a clear statement that *all* education is the elevation of character. This elevation must include every facet of the individual including the spiritual, moral, emotional, intellectual, social, physical and creative. This philosophy must also indicate that prime responsibility for the individual's education rests with the home and that the state and school support that responsibility by providing a curriculum and activities that allow for that growth in all these dimensions. Everything carried out within the state, district, region and school must be related to and based upon that philosophy.

Every public school within the state must display that philosophy. The importance of the philosophy can never be over-emphasized. Thorough examination of it will lead to the resolution of many difficulties that inevitably arise periodically in public education.

Article 2 — Governance

SECTION 1: *MINISTER OF EDUCATION*. Every state shall appoint one individual to oversee the education of all children and young people within its jurisdiction. This individual should be known as the Minister of Education. He or she shall be college educated, have been successful in his or her field of work, have an appreciation of education (both public and private), and have high moral standards. The individual appointed shall not remain in office longer than five years.

The Minister of Education shall appoint separate directors to coordinate and supervise work in the following divisions: administration; finance; selection, training and certification of teachers;

curriculum; student services and standards; buildings and sites; non-public education. These directors shall meet together with the Minister of Education not less than once every three months to monitor progress in all areas. Directors should not remain in office longer than four years. If a Deputy Minister of Education and Assistant Deputies are appointed, they shall not remain in office for more than three years. Continual revitalization of the system is essential for its health. Rotation in office ensures that revitalization and forces individuals to keep abreast of the times. These individuals need to be selected carefully by the Minister of Education to ensure diversity in religion, philosophy and personal beliefs. High standards in professional and personal affairs must be evident in all those selected.

SECTION 2: *BOARDS OF GOVERNORS*. The Minister of Education shall appoint a Board of Governors for every school district within his or her state. These individuals will be the sole governing body for each district and must ensure the district keeps abreast of the times in all educational matters. These people should be carefully selected from the main community or communities within the governed district. They shall not be selected for political, religious or personal reasons. The individuals serving as Board members must be well-educated, have been successful in their own field of work, have an appreciation for public education, and have high moral standards.

Members of the Board of Governors must confine their work to policy-making and not interfere with the daily operation of schools. Operation of the schools must be left to the district Superintendent of Schools and appropriate staff. The following list of duties may be helpful as a guide to new members of each governing body: Ensure that the school system keeps abreast of the times in important educational matters; share leadership in improvements with parents, students, teachers and administrators; be available for consultation with the public, teachers, students, parents and administrators; acquaint the public and all within the system with Board policies and proceedings of a non-confidential nature; exchange ideas with other Board members on important decisions to be made by the Board; help teachers maintain a high professional standing; be alert to the fact that the Board member's primary allegiance is to the public as a whole and not to any political, religious or special interest group; ensure that the Board utilizes federal and state opportunities for financial support; retain control of final decision-making with regard to policy and management of the system, but refrain from involvement in administrative details; be supportive of personnel carrying out Board policies; maintain strict control over all administrative appointments and do not delegate appointments to senior administrators; ensure that Board policies are implemented appropriately and ensure that practices arising from policies are evaluated periodically.

Under no circumstance shall meetings of a Board of Governors be held without all members being notified and invited. If a meeting is held either officially or unofficially without all members invited, the Minister of Education shall be so advised. If after investigation this proves to be the case, that Board shall be dissolved immediately and a new Board appointed.

A Board of Governors may comprise three, five, seven, nine or eleven members, with a balance between ethnic, racial, religious and political groups. A balance should be maintained between male and female members, if possible. Terms of office shall be either two or three years. If the two-year term is chosen by the Minister of Education, Board members shall serve no more than four terms, to a maximum of eight years. If the three-year term is chosen by the Minister of Education, Board members shall serve no more than three terms, to a maximum of nine years. No Board member may be re-appointed to any other School Board throughout the state until the member serving his or her terms has been out of office for at least ten years. An appointment made after a ten-year absence shall be for no more than two two-year terms or one three-year term.

If any Board member fails to carry out his or her duties, the Minister of Education shall remind that person of his or her obligations. If these obligations still remain unmet, the Minister shall immediately replace that member.

Recall of a member of a Board of Governors can be made by the Minister of Education after receiving a petition from at least 10% of the registered voters for a particular school district and after investigating the alleged problems and finding them to be valid. Any member so re-called shall not be appointed again to any school Board of Governors in the state concerned.

Expenses of every Board member shall be borne by the Minister of Education. A tax-free honorarium, with the value to be determined by the Minister of Education, shall be paid monthly to each Board member.

Article 3 — District Administration

SECTION 1: *SUPERINTENDENT OF SCHOOLS.* Administration of each school district within a state shall rest with a chief executive officer to be termed Superintendent of Schools. He or she shall be appointed by the local Board of Governors, and shall report to and be responsible to the Board of Governors of the district concerned. This individual shall also carry out any work assigned by the Minister of Education. Term of office for the position shall be two years for the initial appointment; and if proven satisfactory to the Board of Governors within those two years, appointed for a second term of three years; and if proven satisfactory to the Board of Governors within those three years, appointed to a final term of four years, for a maximum of nine years.

No individual shall be re-appointed Superintendent of Schools within a particular state after completing nine years in that position until he or she has once again taught full-time in the public school system for at least five years. Appointment as a school or district administrator does not constitute appointment as a teacher except for pension and benefit purposes. After completing a full term as Superintendent, that individual must return to a full-time teaching position if he or she wishes to remain within the public education system.

An individual appointed as Superintendent of Schools must be college educated, have an appreciation for education, have high moral standards, have been a successful teacher and successful school administrator, served at least ten years as a full-time school teacher and at least five years as a school administrator. No one shall be appointed Superintendent of Schools, however, who has not served at least three years as a public school principal.

SECTION 2: *SECRETARY-TREASURER*. One secretary-treasurer shall be appointed by the local Board of Governors for every school district within a state. He or she shall report to the Superintendent of Schools and advise both the Superintendent and the local Board of Governors on all matters related to the financial and business operations of the district. The Secretary-Treasurer may be party to discussions and debates on educational issues within the district if the Superintendent of Schools or Board of Governors so decides, but he or she has no voice or vote on decisions to be made on educational issues.

Term of office for the Secretary-Treasurer shall be a renewable three-year term. As this office requires some continuity and as it is a minor office with regard to impact upon the education of the children and young people, it is exempt from the principles of rotation in office and limited terms of appointment. If there is any interference by the Secretary-Treasurer in the harmonious and orderly operation of the school district, he or she shall be reminded by the Minister of Education of his or her obligations to remain separate from the educational aspects of the district. If there is no immediate improvement in this regard, the individual shall be dismissed by the Minister of Education and replaced immediately.

Every Secretary-Treasurer must be college educated, have training in appropriate business and financial practices, have been successful in his or her field of work, have kept abreast of the changes in contemporary technology and accounting practices, have an appreciation of public education, and have high moral standards.

SECTION 3: *ASSISTANT SUPERINTENDENTS*. If the Board of Governors of a school district so decides, it may appoint appropriate Assistant Superintendents for the proper administration of a district. Assistant

Superintendents report directly to the district Superintendent of Schools.

Appointments should be for three years with one renewable term of another three years. No individual may be re-appointed Assistant Superintendent upon completion of six years until he or she has once again taught full-time in a public school for at least five years.

An Assistant Superintendent must be college educated, have an appreciation for education, have been a successful teacher and a successful school administrator with at least ten years as a full-time school teacher and at least five years as a school administrator. No one shall be appointed Assistant Superintendent unless he or she has served at least three years as a public school principal.

SECTION 4: *OTHER ADMINISTRATIVE OFFICERS.* A Board of Governors may appoint other district administrative officers to ensure the proper servicing of the district's education system. These may include Directors of Instruction, Directors of Administration, Directors of Curriculum, Directors of Student Services, Directors of Special Services, Directors of Technology, and others. All of these positions must be for limited terms of office of four to five years and non-renewable except after a return to full-time teaching for at least five years.

No one shall be appointed Director of Instruction, Director of Administration, Director of Curriculum, Director of Student Services, or Director of Special Services without at least ten years of full-time teaching experience. And no one shall be appointed Director of Instruction without at least three years in school administration, where at least two of those three years have been as a public school principal.

Every school district, regardless of enrolment, shall have at least one Director of Instruction. There should be one Director of Instruction up to the first 15,000 students and one Director of Instruction for every 15,000 students after that.

Re-assignment of all administrative officers at the close of their terms shall be to teaching positions.

Requirements for all educational administrative positions are the same. These include a college education, successful teaching and administrative experience, an appreciation for public education, and high moral standards. Graduate study in related fields is desirable but not essential. The essential qualities for all administrators are a desire and an ability to serve — to serve teachers, students, parents, and education itself. It is a desire also to uphold the integrity of public education, an education that must remain apart from political, religious and personal ideologies.

SECTION 5: *SUPPORT STAFF*. Every Board of Governors must select with care all district and school support staff. The main purpose of all support staff is to provide services for the smooth and orderly operation of the schools. All employees must be familiar with and supportive of the district philosophy of character education. They must be models of good character themselves, be cooperative with all, and have high moral standards. They must be competent in their field of work, be well-spoken, and have an affection for children and young people.

Article 4 — School Administration

SECTION 1: *PRINCIPALS*. All teachers within a school district who are qualified, who demonstrate the ability to be an administrator, and who desire to be an administrator, shall have the opportunity somewhere in their career to become a school principal. Administration has become a too-lofty and a too-distant relative of teaching. It cannot exist without teaching. Teaching, on the other hand, can survive without administration. It thrives though when supported and served by an unselfish administration.

It is imperative that teachers do not slip out of teaching to be lost forever in school and district administration, so the practices of rotation in office, limited terms of office, equality of the sexes, equality of opportunity, fairly and universally applied, should be fixed by law and regulation. This will help teaching to remain the focus of all school and district activity.

SECTION 2: *DUTIES.* A principal is responsible for the orderly and harmonious operation of a school. Duties include teachers' timetabling, teaching assignments, placement and promotion of students, supervision of curriculum implementation, textbook use, public relations, extra-curricular government, and any other duty assigned by the Minister of Education and the local Board of Governors.

The principal is responsible for ensuring that the school is run on a purely democratic basis. This means that administrators and teachers work cooperatively for the sound education of the students, an education based totally on elevation of character. The principal must consult with teachers on all matters affecting their work, and shall not interfere with their right to decide on their teaching style, their selection of authorized textbooks and resources, and their communication with all involved in the education of their students. Because ultimate responsibility for administration of the school rests with the principal, the final decision on conflicting matters must rest within the school with the principal. For resolution of irreconcilable differences teachers and principal should consult with the district Superintendent of Schools. The ultimate decision on school-based matters shall remain, however, with the school. At no time should members of the district Board of Governors be involved in the resolution of impasses. The parties involved need to work out their own solutions.

SECTION 3: *ASSISTANT PRINCIPALS.* In every school enrolling at least 100 head count students, an Assistant Principal shall be appointed. The amount of time spent on administration and teaching shall be determined by the Superintendent of Schools in consultation with the Principal of the school concerned. Duties of the Assistant Principal shall be determined by the Principal and shall include assumption of all the Principal's duties in his or her absence.

SECTION 4: *APPOINTMENT.* Principals and Assistant Principals shall be appointed by the district Board of Governors. The Superintendent of Schools, while gathering information on applicants for these positions, may consult with other administrators and any one else he or she may wish in order to get a full picture of the capabilities and character of those applying for these positions. The Superintendent or designate, a teacher representative, a parent representative, and the Board itself shall be the only members of the short-listing and interviewing committee for all administrative positions. The Board alone shall decide upon all appointments.

Equal opportunity must prevail throughout all appointments to ensure that every eligible teacher who applies for these positions realizes fulfilment as an administrator.

Individuals applying for appointment as Assistant Principals and Principals must possess the following qualifications: at least a master's degree in any field of study, highly successful full-time teaching experiences over a period of at least ten years, outstanding organizational abilities, a history of being firm, fair and friendly with students, a record of being cooperative and friendly with others, be an independent thinker, be a tireless worker, have a large capacity for work, have demonstrated a willingness to serve, and have high moral standards.

Terms of office for both Assistant Principal and Principal shall be four to five years each. At the end of a term as Principal individuals shall return to a teaching position within the district.

Article 5 — Teachers

SECTION 1: *SELECTION*. Only individuals recognized as outstanding citizens are eligible for admission to the teaching profession. Individuals wishing to become teachers must apply to a Faculty of Education established within an accredited state public university. It is the responsibility of the applicant to supply evidence of unselfish service to others, to document a history of high moral standards, to document a serious commitment to intellectual pursuits, to supply evidence of an appreciation of and involvement with the artistic or athletic, and to show a willingness to teach others skills and knowledge in these latter areas. The applicant must be thoughtful, respectful, cooperative and principled, a model of the educated citizen. Referees must comment on the applicant's expression of all these attributes.

Every Faculty of Education must establish at least a three-member screening committee to investigate thoroughly the background and eligibility of every applicant. Each committee must be given access to the applicant's university, college, school and work records to determine the suitability of the applicant. Interviews may have to be conducted with appropriate persons to get a full and accurate picture. Interviews must also be conducted with each applicant prior to admission to the Faculty. All accepted must show promising proclivities as teachers of children or young people. No reason shall be given for not accepting a particular applicant, and all information supplied by referees and those interviewed shall remain confidential. The highest ethics shall be observed by those selected to serve on the screening committee in each Faculty of Education.

No one shall be admitted to a Faculty of Education without a bachelor's degree from a recognized college or university. Once admitted to a Faculty of Education the candidate is expected to maintain the high levels of conduct and performance established prior to entrance. These individuals become very quickly one of the prime fashioners of a nation, and as such need to be models of the best society has to offer the world.

SECTION 2: *FACULTIES OF EDUCATION*. Every state should establish and maintain within an accredited degree-granting public college or university a Faculty of Education. Each Faculty of Education shall be staffed at the undergraduate level only with the most outstanding practising teachers and administrators. They must have at least ten years of successful teaching experience in public schools. They must also have a record of service to their students, be skilful teachers in their own subject areas, be ideal models for prospective teachers to emulate, and have high moral standards. Appointments shall be for no longer than three years, at the end of which individuals shall return to their own teaching positions in the schools.

Each Faculty of Education shall offer a two-year programme, at the end of which successful candidates are granted the degree of Bachelor of Education. No distinction is to be made in length of programme for those planning to teach in either elementary school or secondary school. At least three months in each of the two years shall be spent in teaching within state schools. The majority of instruction within each Faculty of Education shall be on teaching styles, techniques and approaches, but time must be set aside for a thorough examination of character education and how it is achieved in practical ways within the schools. Each Faculty of Education must be viewed as a professional institution designed to prepare the highly qualified candidate not in an academic way, which has already been done through college or university training, but in practical day to day teaching duties and assignments. Faculties of Education are not academic institutions; they are professional institutions.

Selection of staff at the graduate level in each Faculty of Education does not have to be done as rigorously as that at the undergraduate level. Advanced work here is more on a technical and theoretical level in specialized areas such as curriculum, counselling, administration, special education, technology, and so forth, so instructors and professors seldom fashion the thinking and feeling of their students to the degree done at the undergraduate level. Individuals selected here are chosen more for their technical expertise than for their character, which should of course be at least noteworthy.

SECTION 3: *COLLEGE OF TEACHERS*. Every state should establish and maintain its own College of Teachers. Each College should admit to its ranks those individuals granted the Bachelor of Education by appropriate colleges and universities. Each College should be governed by its own members, with advisory roles given to representatives of the Minister of Education and each Faculty of Education within a state. The College shall not establish any rules or procedures that contravene state legislation governing education.

The purposes of the College are to certify individuals to teach, to ensure high standards of professional conduct, and to discipline its own members when necessary. Members of the College and the Minister of Education are responsible for the financing of its operations.

SECTION 4: *TEACHING.* Every teacher is responsible for the total education of every pupil under his or her instruction. This must include provision for spiritual, moral, emotional, intellectual, creative, social and physical development. While attention is normally not focused on any single area at one specific time, an awareness and provision for growth in all areas are essential at all times.

In the absence of the parents or guardians the teacher is the primary authority in the school for the pupils under his or her instruction. He or she may consult with the Principal, Assistant Principal or other teachers, but these individuals do not replace or usurp the teacher's authority to decide on the learning activities and the control and discipline of those pupils. If there is reason to question the teacher's judgment in these matters, the Principal must report to the Superintendent of Schools on that judgment and the Superintendent and at least two other teachers examine the areas of concern.

Teachers, Principal and Assistant Principals should advise parents on the standard of conduct and performance expected in the school and at all its functions. Teachers should consult with parents periodically to ensure there is consistency and fairness in the treatment of pupils. Teachers must be consistently firm, fair and friendly in their dealings with all pupils.

Wherever possible, appropriate transfer of teachers shall take place so that no teacher remains in the same school longer than ten years. This will help prevent teacher stagnation.

Article 6 — Curriculum

SECTION 1: *SCHOOL ORGANIZATION.* The ideal organization of schools to further character education should keep students together within a broad chronological age grouping. The ideal is to have Kindergarten or Grade 1 through Grade 5 in one group of buildings (Primary School); the next group from Grade 6 through Grade 8 (Middle School) in another group of buildings; and the third group from Grade 9 through Grade 12 (High School) in a third group of buildings. This gives broad, relatively compatible, age groupings of 5–10, 11–13, 14–18 years of age. The arrangement helps basically to have children remain children as long as possible by constant contact with those of their own age and interests.

SECTION 2: *CURRICULUM*. It is important to remember when establishing the curriculum for all these age groups that it is simply the avenue for the development of character. The curriculum needs to be content-filled. The teacher uncovers the content in keeping with the abilities of the children taught. There is no need to rush into that content at an early age, nor speed through it at various ages. Movement through all content for skills, knowledge and appreciation should be gradual, unhurried.

Emphasis on gradual movement does not rule out the use of examinations and assignments to determine levels of skill, knowledge and appreciation. Neither does it preclude the introduction of numerous elective courses at the High School level.

The extra-curricular offerings need also to be full and complementary to the basic curriculum. These all enrich the opportunities for character development and must be planned by state and local authorities.

SECTION 3: *TEXTBOOKS*. Textbooks and resource materials should be state controlled and up-dated regularly by the state. The Minister of Education must approve, have published, and issue all textbooks used in public schools as part of the Ministry-approved curriculum. All major resource materials used with the curriculum must be approved by the Ministry. Minor materials for these courses and locally-developed courses should not require Ministry approval.

Article 7 — Finance

SECTION 1: *STATE FUNDING*. Funds for all public schools within a state shall be allocated solely by the state government. These funds shall be collected by both state and federal governments from varied sources. Revenue sources will vary from country to country, but they will usually include residential property taxes, commercial property taxes, sales taxes and income taxes. It should also include a special education tax. The principle of encouraging every citizen, regardless of possession or lack of possession of property or belongings, to pay for the education of a nation's children and youth is important in a democratic society. This includes financing the establishment, maintenance and modernization of all public schools within a state.

Federal governments, while not involved in the governance of education within each state within their nation, need to collect and allocate funds to education in each state on an equitable basis. The primary purpose of this is to ensure equity in the quality of education throughout the nation. State governments need to allocate funds to ensure equalization throughout their states, so education in remote regions is comparable, even though slightly different, from that received in major centres of the state. Allowance must be made for wide variations in local conditions.

No federal, state or local funds shall be given to parochial, private, dissentient, denominational, separate, independent or non-governmental schools.

Under no circumstances shall school boards, school districts or municipal bodies be permitted to raise funds through local taxation for the operation of their schools.

SECTION 2: *CONTINGENCY FUND*. Every school district shall be given at start-up a contingency fund equal to 10% of its initial operating budget. Monies for this fund shall be deposited in a savings account within the school district, and the initial capital shall not be depleted in any way during the existence of the school district. Monies may be added at any time. The monies earned from the interest may be used by the School Board in any way it wishes.

SECTION 3: *SALARIES*. Teachers' salaries shall be negotiated on a state basis between a chief negotiator for an employers' association

77

representing all school boards in a state and the state government, and a chief negotiator for the state teachers' organization. Both negotiators may include representatives from their respective bodies, but in no case shall this number be larger than twenty-one members for each group. Principal and Assistant Principals shall have a representative on the teachers' unit. They may or may not be members of the teachers' organization but every Principal and Assistant Principal shall pay an annual fee to the teachers' organization to help defray expenses involved in negotiations.

Negotiations shall begin four months prior to the expiry of each contract. If no agreement is reached within the first eight weeks, a mediator shall be selected from a list of professional mediators acceptable to both chief negotiators. If no agreement is reached by the end of the twelfth week, the items still in dispute shall be referred to a three-member arbitration board, with one arbitrator chosen by the teachers' group, one chosen by the employers' association and the third member (to serve as chairman) chosen by the two arbitrators. Arbitration shall not be final offer arbitration, but it shall be binding on both parties and shall be concluded before the expiry of the current contract.

All contracts shall be for at least two years.

Neither lock-outs, strikes nor disruptive actions shall be allowed to interfere with the education of a state's children and youth.

All costs for negotiation, mediation and arbitration shall be borne by the Minister of Education.

All salaries, allowances and working conditions for teachers, principals and assistant principals are negotiable.

Under no circumstances shall salaries and allowances for principals and assistant principals or any other school-based administrator be in excess of the maximum salary for teachers within a state.

Under no circumstances shall salaries and allowances for superintendents of schools and assistant superintendents be in excess of the maximum salary for teachers within a state.

Under no circumstances shall salaries and allowances for other district educational administrative officers, and others, be in excess of the maximum salary for teachers within a state.

Under no circumstances shall salaries and allowances for the secretary-treasurer or any other business administration officer or support staff be in excess of the maximum salary for teachers within a state.

Salaries for men and women in all categories shall be identical.

Article 8 — Student and Parent Responsibilities

SECTION 1: *PREPARATION.* It is the responsibility of parents to ensure their children attend school every day prepared to learn. This includes daily attendance for the full school day, punctuality, and an application to studies and activities planned by teachers. It also includes ensuring compliance with school rules and regulations and standards of conduct. These include respect for all and civility in dealings with other students, with teachers, with administrators, and with all others supporting the schools. It also includes carrying out in a reasonable manner all work assigned. Under no circumstances shall revenge or retaliation be permitted in schools. And under no circumstances shall there be any profanity, vulgarity, pornography, drugs, alcohol, vandalism or violence within a school or on school premises or at a school-run function.

SECTION 2: *RESPONSIBILITY.* If a student fails to comply with the school rules, regulations and standards of conduct, he or she shall be removed from the school and become the sole responsibility of the parents.

SECTION 3: *PEACE AND ORDER.* It is imperative that all students learn in a peaceful atmosphere. And it is incumbent upon administrators, teachers and parents to ensure that nothing disrupts that atmosphere. If there is a major disruption, Principals are authorized by law to call upon a constable or a peace-keeping officer to restore that atmosphere and remove if necessary any individual causing a disturbance.

SECTION 4: *PERFORMANCE*. All students are expected to perform to the best of their ability in every course and activity. Evaluation of performance shall be conducted annually in grades 5, 8 and 12 in the academic areas of the native language, history and geography, mathematics and science. State examinations shall be conducted annually in all major academic areas in the graduating year. Evaluation shall be made annually in the spring of every student throughout the state not attending a public school or a non-public school. This evaluation shall be conducted by the Principal of the nearest public school in the district in which such a student resides. The evaluation shall be of the total growth and development of the student.

SECTION 5: *REPORTING TO PARENTS*. All student progress reports shall be in the form of comments for the entire Primary School years. Reports for the Middle School and High School years shall be in the form of letter grades and comments. Wherever possible comments should indicate development along physical, social, emotional, creative, mental, moral and spiritual lines.

Article 9 — Transportation and Housing

SECTION 1: *ACCOMMODATION*. In isolated or remote regions of a state accommodation for all teachers and administrators shall be provided at a reasonable rate. Full costs of maintenance of the accommodation shall be borne by the Minister of Education.

SECTION 2: *TRANSPORTATION*. Transportation shall be provided by district School Boards for all students living beyond four kilometres from their neighbourhood school. In certain cases this may be in the form of reimbursement for travel costs.

A school bus of appropriate size shall be stationed permanently at every remote or isolated school having access to a road or roads that lead to larger cultural centres. This bus shall be for the sole use of the school and shall not be used by other community groups. Only fully licensed bus drivers shall operate such a bus. Safety checks of every school bus must be made every month of operation.

Article 10 — Buildings and Grounds

SECTION 1: *SCHOOL BUILDINGS*. The Minister of Education for every state shall have in place a plan for the construction, renewal and replacement of all schools within the state. It shall include plans for the modernization and replacement of structures every fifty to sixty years. All buildings must be kept abreast of the times and be contemporary and attractive in design and construction. They must also be practical and functional, and be able to incorporate the latest in technology and relevant inventions. Students, teachers and administrators must be kept on the cutting edge of human progress. Keeping buildings up to date is part of that progress.

SECTION 2: *SCHOOL SITES*. The Board of Governors for every school district must secure well in advance sites for the construction and replacement of all schools within their jurisdiction. This must include an abundance of outdoor playing surface. Expropriation of surrounding properties and buildings may have to be undertaken to guarantee this abundance. Appropriate replacement property and buildings shall be found for those having property and buildings expropriated. All sites must be attractively landscaped upon completion of new buildings and grounds.

SECTION 3: *BUILDING AND SITE COORDINATION*. The Minister of Education shall maintain a central department dealing solely with school buildings and sites throughout a state. This department shall be responsible, through the Minister of Education, for the coordination of expropriation, construction, renewal and funding for all school capital projects. A master plan of all buildings and sites and plans for their renewal shall be maintained by this department.

All capital projects shall be financed by the Minister of Education.

Index

Language
aboriginal, native, heritage 18
national 17, 19, 21, 80
second 18, 19, 24
Law 13, 18, 27, 49, 54, 55, 63, 64, 70
Leader,
as an administrator 38
educational 39
as a teacher 35
youth 35
Learning 36, 44, 45
disruption of 11
formal 16
speed of 26
styles 33
weakness 28
Lecturing, as a teaching method 34
Leniency 12
Liberty, religious 54
Library, school 24
Life-style 7, 29
education 28
Lincoln, Abraham 53
Listening, as a teaching method 34
as communication 18
Literature 20, 25
religious 55
Lock-outs 78
London 1
Love 10, 16, 28
of good 4, 26
of one another 4, 12, 45
Lust 9

Lying 59, 60
Majority rule 53
Male, Board members 66
Management, consultants 55
courses 27
policy 66
Managers 38
Managua 1
Mankind 10
Manuals, as resources 20
Markets 27
Market-place 20
Marriage 13, 45
education 30
Mathematics 12, 18, 19, 21, 25, 80
Measurement, of intellectual
abilities 10
of progress 9
Medicine 18
Media 30
Meditation 27, 28
Memory, as a teaching
method 34
Men's and women's salaries 79
Mental, deformity 7
development 17, 80
dimensions 2, 3, 10, 21
stability 8
state 7
Mentoring, as a teaching method 34
Mentors 31
Mercy 10, 19, 23
Metis 28
Mildness 10
Mind, and school philosophy 4